Charles Scribner Jr.
1939.

THE MIND IN THE MAKING

The Relation of Intelligence to Social Reform

By

JAMES HARVEY ROBINSON

Author of
"PETRARCH, THE FIRST MODERN SCHOLAR"
"MEDIÆVAL AND MODERN TIMES"
"THE NEW HISTORY," ETC.

HARPER & BROTHERS PUBLISHERS
NEW YORK AND LONDON

THE MIND IN THE MAKING

Copyright, 1921, by Harper & Brothers
Printed in the United States of America

G-N

CONTENTS

I

	PAGE
Preface	vii
1. On the Purpose of This Volume	3
2. Three Disappointed Methods of Reform	14

II

3. On Various Kinds of Thinking	33
4. Rationalizing	40
5. How Creative Thought Transforms the World	48

III

6. Our Animal Heritage. The Nature of Civilization	65
7. Our Savage Mind	81

IV

8. Beginning of Critical Thinking	97
9. Influence of Plato and Aristotle	106

V

10. Origin of Mediæval Civilization	117
11. Our Mediæval Intellectual Inheritance	123

CONTENTS

VI

		PAGE
12.	THE SCIENTIFIC REVOLUTION	151
13.	HOW SCIENTIFIC KNOWLEDGE HAS REVOLUTIONIZED THE CONDITIONS OF LIFE	158

VII

| 14. | "THE SICKNESS OF AN ACQUISITIVE SOCIETY" | 171 |
| 15. | THE PHILOSOPHY OF SAFETY AND SANITY | 179 |

VIII

16.	SOME REFLECTIONS ON THE PHILOSOPHY OF REPRESSION	197
17.	WHAT OF IT?	211
	APPENDIX	231

PREFACE

This is an essay—not a treatise—on the most important of all matters of human concern. Although it has cost its author a great deal more thought and labor than will be apparent, it falls, in his estimation, far below the demands of its implacably urgent theme. Each page could readily be expanded into a volume. It suggests but the beginning of the beginning now being made to raise men's thinking onto a plain which may perhaps enable them to fend off or reduce some of the dangers which lurk on every hand.

J. H. R.

New School for Social Research,
 New York City,
 August, 1921.

I

Now, my thesis is that all . . . fugues from actuality and what Desjardin made supreme, *viz.*, *le devoir présent*, are now, as never before in history, weak and cowardly flights from the duty of the hour, wasteful of precious energy, and, perhaps worst of all, they are a symptom of low morale, personal or civic, or both. True greatness consists solely in seeing everything, past, future or afar, in terms of the Here and Now, or in the power of "presentification."—G. STANLEY HALL.

THE MIND IN THE MAKING

1. On the Purpose of This Volume

IF some magical transformation could be produced in men's ways of looking at themselves and their fellows, no inconsiderable part of the evils which now afflict society would vanish away or remedy themselves automatically. If the majority of influential persons held the opinions and occupied the point of view that a few rather uninfluential people now do, there would, for instance, be no likelihood of another great war; the whole problem of "labor and capital" would be transformed and attenuated; national arrogance, race animosity, political corruption, and inefficiency would all be reduced below the danger point. As an old Stoic proverb has it, men are tormented by the opinions they have of things, rather than by the things themselves. This is eminently true of many of our worst problems to-day. We have available knowledge and ingenuity and material resources to make a far fairer world than that in which we find ourselves, but various obstacles prevent our intelligently availing ourselves of them. The object of this book is to substantiate this proposition, to exhibit with entire frankness the tremendous difficulties that stand in the way of such a beneficent change of mind, and to point out as clearly as may be some of the measures to be taken in order to overcome them.

When we contemplate the shocking derangement of human affairs which now prevails in most civilized countries, including our own, even the best minds are puzzled and uncertain in their attempts to grasp the situation. The world seems to demand a moral and economic regeneration which it is dangerous to postpone, but as yet impossible to imagine, let alone direct. The preliminary intellectual regeneration which would put our leaders in a position to determine and control the course of affairs has not taken place. We have unprecedented conditions to deal with and novel adjustments to make—there can be no doubt of that. We also have a great stock of scientific knowledge unknown to our grandfathers with which to operate. So novel are the conditions, so copious the knowledge, that we must undertake the arduous task of reconsidering a great part of the opinions about man and his relations to his fellow-men which have been handed down to us by previous generations who lived in far other conditions and possessed far less information about the world and themselves. We have, however, first to create an *unprecedented attitude of mind to cope with unprecedented conditions, and to utilize unprecedented knowledge*. This is the preliminary, and most difficult, step to be taken—far more difficult than one would suspect who fails to realize that in order to take it we must overcome inveterate natural tendencies and artificial habits of long standing. How are we to put ourselves in a position to come to think of things that we not only never thought of before, but are most reluctant to question? In short, how are we to rid ourselves of our fond prejudices and *open our minds?*

As a historical student who for a good many years has been especially engaged in inquiring how man happens to have the ideas and convictions about himself and human relations which now prevail, the writer has reached the conclusion that history can at least shed a great deal of light on our present predicaments and confusion. I do not mean by history that conventional chronicle of remote and irrelevant events which embittered the youthful years of many of us, but rather a study of how man has come to be as he is and to believe as he does.

No historian has so far been able to make the whole story very plain or popular, but a number of considerations are obvious enough, and it ought not to be impossible some day to popularize them. I venture to think that if certain seemingly indisputable historical facts were generally known and accepted and permitted to play a daily part in our thought, the world would forthwith become a very different place from what it now is. We could then neither delude ourselves in the simple-minded way we now do, nor could we take advantage of the primitive ignorance of others. All our discussions of social, industrial, and political reform would be raised to a higher plane of insight and fruitfulness.

In one of those brilliant divagations with which Mr. H. G. Wells is wont to enrich his novels he says:

> When the intellectual history of this time comes to be written, nothing, I think, will stand out more strikingly than the empty gulf in quality between the superb and richly fruitful scientific investigations that are going on, and the general thought of other educated sections of the community. I do not mean that scientific men are, as a whole, a class of supermen, dealing with and thinking about everything in a way altogether better than the common run of humanity,

ON THE PURPOSE OF THIS VOLUME

but in their field they think and work with an intensity, an integrity, a breadth, boldness, patience, thoroughness, and faithfulness—excepting only a few artists—which puts their work out of all comparison with any other human activity. . . . In these particular directions the human mind has achieved a new and higher quality of attitude and gesture, a veracity, a self-detachment, and self-abnegating vigor of criticism that tend to spread out and must ultimately spread out to every other human affair.

No one who is even most superficially acquainted with the achievements of students of nature during the past few centuries can fail to see that their thought has been astoundingly effective in constantly adding to our knowledge of the universe, from the hugest nebula to the tiniest atom; moreover, this knowledge has been so applied as to well-nigh revolutionize human affairs, and both the knowledge and its applications appear to be no more than hopeful beginnings, with indefinite revelations ahead, if only the same kind of thought be continued in the same patient and scrupulous manner.

But the knowledge of man, of the springs of his conduct, of his relation to his fellow-men singly or in groups, and the felicitous regulation of human intercourse in the interest of harmony and fairness, have made no such advance. Aristotle's treatises on astronomy and physics, and his notions of "generation and decay" and of chemical processes, have long gone by the board, but his politics and ethics are still revered. Does this mean that his penetration in the sciences of man exceeded so greatly his grasp of natural science, or does it mean that the progress of mankind in the scientific knowledge and regulation of human affairs has remained almost stationary for over two thousand years? I think that we may safely conclude that the latter is the case. It has required three centuries of scientific thought and of subtle inventions for its promotion to enable a modern chemist or physicist to center his attention on electrons and their relation to the mysterious nucleus of the atom, or to permit an embryologist to study the early stirrings of the fertilized egg. As yet relatively little of the same kind of thought has been brought to bear on human affairs.

When we compare the discussions in the United States Senate in regard to the League of Nations with the consideration of a broken-down car in a roadside garage the contrast is shocking. The rural mechanic thinks scientifically; his only aim is to avail himself of his knowledge of the nature and workings of the car, with a view to making it run once more. The Senator, on the other hand, appears too often to have little idea of the nature and workings of nations, and he relies on rhetoric and appeals to vague fears and hopes or mere partisan animosity. The scientists have been busy for a century in revolutionizing the *practical* relation of nations. The ocean is no longer a barrier, as it was in Washington's day, but to all intents and purposes a smooth avenue closely connecting, rather than safely separating, the eastern and western continents. The Senator will nevertheless unblushingly appeal to policies of a century back, suitable, mayhap, in their day, but now become a warning rather than a guide. The garage man, on the contrary, takes his mechanism as he finds it, and does not allow any mystic respect for the earlier forms of the gas engine to interfere with the needed adjustments.

Those who have dealt with natural phenomena, as distinguished from purely human concerns, did not, however, quickly or easily gain popular approbation and respect. The process of emancipating natural science from current prejudices, both of the learned and of the unlearned, has been long and painful, and is not wholly completed yet. If we go back to the opening of the seventeenth century we find three men whose business it was, above all, to present and defend common sense in the natural sciences. The most eloquent and variedly persuasive of these was Lord Bacon. Then there was the young Descartes trying to shake himself loose from his training in a Jesuit seminary by going into the Thirty Years' War, and starting his intellectual life all over by giving up for the moment all he had been taught. Galileo had committed an offense of a grave character by discussing in the mother tongue the problems of physics. In his old age he was imprisoned and sentenced to repeat the seven penitential psalms for differing from Aristotle and Moses and the teachings of the theologians. On hearing Galileo's fate, Descartes burned a book he had written, *On the World*, lest he, too, get into trouble.

From that time down to the days of Huxley and John Fiske the struggle has continued, and still continues—the Three Hundred Years' War for intellectual freedom in dealing with natural phenomena. It has been a conflict against ignorance, tradition, and vested interests in church and university, with all that preposterous invective and cruel misrepresentation which characterize the fight against new and critical ideas. Those who cried out against scientific discoveries did so in the wont to explain and sanctify his ways, with little regard to their fundamental and permanent expediency. An arresting example of what this muddling may mean we have seen during these recent years in the slaying or maiming of fifteen million of our young men, resulting in incalculable loss, continued disorder, and bewilderment. Yet men seem blindly driven to defend and perpetuate the conditions which produced the last disaster.

Unless we wish to see a recurrence of this or some similar calamity, we must, as I have already suggested, create a new and unprecedented attitude of mind to meet the new and unprecedented conditions which confront us. *We should proceed to the thorough reconstruction of our mind, with a view to understanding actual human conduct and organization.* We must examine the facts freshly, critically, and dispassionately, and then allow our philosophy to formulate itself as a result of this examination, instead of permitting our observations to be distorted by archaic philosophy, political economy, and ethics. As it is, we are taught our philosophy first, and in its light we try to justify the facts. We must reverse this process, as did those who began the great work in experimental science; we must first face the facts, and patiently await the emergence of a new philosophy.

A willingness to examine the very foundations of society does not mean a desire to encourage or engage in any hasty readjustment, but certainly no wise or needed readjustment *can* be made unless such an examination is undertaken.

I come back, then, to my original point that in this examination of existing facts history, by revealing the origin of many of our current fundamental beliefs, will tend to free our minds so as to permit honest thinking. Also, that the historical facts which I propose to recall would, if permitted to play a constant part in our thinking, automatically eliminate a very considerable portion of the gross stupidity and blindness which characterize our present thought and conduct in public affairs, and would contribute greatly to developing the needed scientific attitude toward human concerns—in other words, to *bringing the mind up to date*.

2. Three Disappointed Methods of Reform

Plans for social betterment and the cure of public ills have in the past taken three general forms: (I) changes in the rules of the game, (II) spiritual exhortation, and (III) education. Had all these not largely failed, the world would not be in the plight in which it now confessedly is.

I. Many reformers concede that they are suspicious of what they call "ideas." They are confident that our troubles result from defective organization, which should be remedied by more expedient legislation and wise ordinances. Abuses should be abolished or checked by forbidding them, or by some ingenious reordering of procedure. Responsibility should be concentrated or dispersed. The term of office of government officials should be lengthened or shortened; the number of members in governing bodies should be increased or decreased; there should be direct primaries, referendum, recall, government by commission; powers should be shifted here and there with a hope of meeting obvious mischances all too familiar in the past. In industry and education administrative reform is constantly going on, with the hope of reducing friction and increasing efficiency. The House of Commons not long ago came to new terms with the peers. The League of Nations has already had to adjust the functions and influence of the Council and the Assembly, respectively.

No one will question that organization is

absolutely essential in human affairs, but reorganization, while it sometimes produces assignable benefit, often fails to meet existing evils, and not uncommonly engenders new and unexpected ones. Our confidence in restriction and regimentation is exaggerated. What we usually need is a *change of attitude*, and without this our new regulations often leave the old situation unaltered. So long as we allow our government to be run by politicians and business lobbies it makes little difference how many aldermen or assemblymen we have or how long the mayor or governor holds office. In a university the fundamental drift of affairs cannot be greatly modified by creating a new dean, or a university council, or by enhancing or decreasing the nominal authority of the president or faculty. We now turn to the second sanctified method of reform, moral uplift.

II. Those who are impatient with mere administrative reform, or who lack faith in it, declare that what we need is brotherly love. Thousands of pulpits admonish us to remember that we are all children of one Heavenly Father and that we should bear one another's burdens with fraternal patience. Capital is too selfish; Labor is bent on its own narrow interests regardless of the risks Capital takes.

We are all dependent on one another, and a recognition of this should beget mutual forbearance and glad co-operation. Let us forget ourselves in others. "Little children, love one another."

The fatherhood of God has been preached by Christians for over eighteen centuries, and the brotherhood of man by the Stoics long before them. The doctrine has proved compatible with slavery and serfdom, with wars blessed, and not infrequently instigated, by religious leaders, and with industrial oppression which it requires a brave clergyman or teacher to denounce to-day. True, we sometimes have moments of sympathy when our fellow-creatures become objects of tender solicitude. Some rare souls may honestly flatter themselves that they love mankind in general, but it would surely be a very rare soul indeed who dared profess that he loved his personal enemies—much less the enemies of his country or institutions. We still worship a tribal god, and the "foe" is not to be reckoned among his children. Suspicion and hate are much more congenial to our natures than love, for very obvious reasons in this world of rivalry and common failure. There is, beyond doubt, a natural kindliness in mankind which will show itself under favorable auspices. But experience would seem to teach that it is little promoted by moral exhortation. This is the only point that need be urged here. Whether there is another way of forwarding the brotherhood of man will be considered in the sequel.

III. One disappointed in the effects of mere reorganization, and distrusting the power of moral exhortation, will urge that what we need above all is *education*. It is quite true that what we need is education, but something so different from what now passes as such that it needs a new name.

Education has more various aims than we usually recognize, and should of course be judged in relation to the importance of its several intentions, and of its success in gaining them. The arts of reading and writing and figuring all would concede are basal in a world of newspapers and business. Then there is technical information and the training that prepares one to earn a livelihood in some more or less standardized guild or profession. Both these aims are reached fairly well by our present educational system, subject to various economies and improvements in detail. Then there are the studies which it is assumed contribute to general culture and to "training the mind," with the hope of cultivating our tastes, stimulating the imagination, and mayhap improving our reasoning powers.

This branch of education is regarded by the few as very precious and indispensable; by the many as at best an amenity which has little relation to the real purposes and success of life. It is highly traditional and retrospective in the main, concerned with ancient tongues, old and revered books, higher mathematics, somewhat archaic philosophy and history, and the fruitless form of logic which has until recently been prized as man's best guide in the fastnesses of error. To these has been added in recent decades a choice of the various branches of natural science.

The results, however, of our present scheme of liberal education are disappointing. One who, like myself, firmly agrees with its objects and is personally so addicted to old books, so pleased with such knowledge as he has of the ancient and modern languages, so envious of those who can think mathematically, and so interested in natural science—such a person must resent the fact that those who have had a liberal education rarely care for old books, rarely read for pleasure any foreign language, think mathematically, love philosophy or history, or care for the beasts, birds, plants, and rocks with any intelligent insight, or even real curiosity. This arouses the suspicion that our so-called "liberal education" miscarries and does not attain its ostensible aims.

The three educational aims enumerated above have one thing in common. They are all directed toward an enhancement of the chances of *personal* worldly success, or to the increase of our *personal* culture and intellectual and literary enjoyment. Their purpose is not primarily to fit us to play a part in social or political betterment. But of late a fourth element has been added to the older ambitions, namely the hope of preparing boys and girls to become intelligent voters. This need has been forced upon us by the coming of political democracy, which makes one person's vote exactly as good as another's.

Now education for citizenship would seem to consist in gaining a knowledge of the actual workings of our social organization, with some illuminating notions of its origin, together with a full realization of its defects and their apparent sources. But here we encounter an obstacle that is unimportant in the older types of education, but which may prove altogether fatal to any good results in our efforts to make better citizens. Subjects of instruction like reading and writing, mathematics, Latin and Greek, chemistry and physics, medicine and the law are fairly well standardized and retrospective. Doubtless there is a good deal of internal change in method and content going on, but this takes place unobtrusively and does not attract the attention of outside critics. Political and social questions, on the other hand, and matters relating to prevailing business methods, race animosities, public elections, and governmental policy are, if they are vital, necessarily "controversial." School boards and superintendents, trustees and presidents of colleges and universities, are sensitive to this fact. They eagerly deprecate in their public manifestos any suspicion that pupils and students are being awakened in any way to the truth that our institutions can possibly be fundamentally defective, or that the present generation of citizens has not conducted our affairs with exemplary success, guided by the immutable principles of justice.

How indeed can a teacher be expected to explain to the sons and daughters of business men, politicians, doctors, lawyers, and clergymen—all pledged to the maintenance of the sources of their livelihood—the actual nature of business enterprise as now practiced, the prevailing methods of legislative bodies and courts, and the conduct of foreign affairs? Think of a teacher in the public schools recounting the more illuminating facts about the municipal government under which he lives, with due attention to graft and jobs! So, courses in government, political economy, sociology, and ethics confine themselves to inoffensive generalizations, harmless details of organization, and the commonplaces of routine morality, for only in that way can they escape being controversial. Teachers are rarely able or inclined to explain our social life and its presuppositions with sufficient insight and honesty to produce any very important results. Even if they are tempted to tell the essential facts they dare not do so, for fear of losing their places, amid the applause of all the righteously minded.

However we may feel on this important matter, we must all agree that the aim of education for citizenship as now conceived is a preparation for the same old citizenship which has so far failed to eliminate the shocking hazards and crying injustices of our social and political life. For we sedulously inculcate in the coming generation exactly the same illusions and the same ill-placed confidence in existing institutions and prevailing notions that have brought the world to the pass in which we find it. Since we do all we can to corroborate the beneficence of what we have, we can hardly hope to raise up a more intelligent generation bent on achieving what we have not. We all know this to be true; it has been forcibly impressed on our minds of late. Most of us agree that it is right and best that it should be so; some of us do not like to think about it at all, but a few will be glad to spend a little time weighing certain suggestions in this volume which may indicate a way out of this *impasse*.[1]

We have now considered briefly the three main hopes that have been hitherto entertained of bettering things, (I) by changing the rules of the game, (II) by urging men to be good, and to love their neighbor as themselves, and (III) by education for citizenship. It may be that these hopes are not wholly unfounded, but it must be admitted that so far they have been grievously disappointed. Doubtless they will continue to be cherished on account of their assured respectability.

---

[1] George Bernard Shaw reaches a similar conclusion when he contemplates education in the British Isles. "We must teach citizenship and political science at school. But must we? There is no must about it, the hard fact being that we must *not* teach political science or citizenship at school. The schoolmaster who attempted it would soon find himself penniless in the streets without pupils, if not in the dock pleading to a pompously worded indictment for sedition against the exploiters. Our schools teach the morality of feudalism corrupted by commercialism, and hold up the military conqueror, the robber baron, and the profiteer, as models of the illustrious and successful."—*Back to Methuselah*, xii.

Mere lack of success does not discredit a method, for there are many things that determine and perpetuate our sanctified ways of doing things besides their success in reaching their proposed ends. Had this not always been so, our life to-day would be far less stupidly conducted than it is. But let us agree to assume for the moment that the approved schemes of reform enumerated above have, to say the least, shown themselves inadequate to meet the crisis in which civilized society now finds itself. Have we any other hope?

Yes, there is Intelligence. That is as yet an untested hope in its application to the regulation of human relations. It is not discredited because it has not been tried on any large scale outside the realm of natural science. There, everyone will confess, it has produced marvelous results. Employed in regard to stars, rocks, plants, and animals, and in the investigation of mechanical and chemical processes, it has completely revolutionized men's notions of the world in which they live, and of its inhabitants, *with the notable exception of man himself.* These discoveries have been used to change our habits and to supply us with everyday necessities which a hundred years ago were not dreamed

THREE METHODS OF REFORM

of as luxuries accessible even to kings and millionaires.

But most of us know too little of the past to realize the penalty that had to be paid for this application of intelligence. In order that these discoveries should be made and ingeniously applied to the conveniences of life, *it was necessary to discard practically all the consecrated notions of the world and its workings which had been held by the best and wisest and purest of mankind down to three hundred years ago*—indeed, until much more recently. Intelligence, in a creature of routine like man and in a universe so ill understood as ours, must often break valiantly with the past in order to get ahead. It would be pleasant to assume that all we had to do was to build on well-designed foundations, firmly laid by the wisdom of the ages. But those who have studied the history of natural science would agree that Bacon, Galileo, and Descartes found no such foundation, but had to begin their construction from the ground up.

The several hopes of reform mentioned above all assume that the now generally accepted notions of righteous human conduct are not to be questioned. Our churches and universities defend this assumption. Our editors and lawyers and the more vocal of our business men adhere to it. Even those who pretend to study society and its origin seem often to believe that our present ideals and standards of property, the state, industrial organization, the relations of the sexes, and education are practically final and must necessarily be the basis of any possible betterment in detail. But if this be so Intelligence has already done its perfect work, and we can only lament that the outcome in the way of peace, decency, and fairness, judged even by existing standards, has been so disappointing.

There are, of course, a few here and there who suspect and even repudiate current ideals and standards. But at present their resentment against existing evils takes the form of more or less dogmatic plans of reconstruction, like those of the socialists and communists, or exhausts itself in the vague protest and faultfinding of the average "Intellectual." Neither the socialist nor the common run of Intellectual appears to me to be on the right track. The former is more precise in his doctrines and confident in his prophecies than a scientific examination of mankind and its ways would at all justify; the other, more indefinite than he need be.

If Intelligence is to have the freedom of action necessary to accumulate new and valuable knowledge about man's nature and possibilities which may ultimately be applied to reforming our ways, it must loose itself from the bonds that now confine it. The primeval curse still holds: "Of every tree in the garden thou mayest freely eat; but of the tree of the knowledge of good and evil, thou shalt not eat of it; for in the day that thou eatest thereof thou shalt surely die." Few people confess that they are afraid of knowledge, but the university presidents, ministers, and editors who most often and publicly laud what they are wont to call "the fearless pursuit of truth," feel compelled, in the interest of public morals and order, to discourage any reckless indulgence in the fruit of the forbidden tree, for the inexperienced may select an unripe apple and suffer from the colic in consequence. "Just look at Russia!" Better always, instead of taking the risk on what the church calls "science falsely so called," fall back on ignorance rightly so called. No one denies that Intelligence is the light of the world and the chief glory of man, but, as Bertrand Russell says, we dread its indifference to respectable opinions and what we deem the well-tried wisdom of the ages. "It is," as he truly says, "fear that holds men back; fear that their cherished beliefs should prove harmful, fear lest they themselves should prove less worthy of respect than they have supposed themselves to be. 'Should the workingman think freely about property? What then will become of us, the rich? Should young men and women think freely about sex? What then will become of morality? Should soldiers think freely about war? What then will become of military discipline?'"

This fear is natural and inevitable, but it is none the less dangerous and discreditable. Human arrangements are no longer so foolproof as they may once have been when the world moved far more slowly than it now does. It should therefore be a good deed to remove or lighten any of the various restraints on thought. I believe that there is an easy and relatively painless way in which our respect for the past can be lessened so that we shall no longer feel compelled to take the wisdom of the ages as the basis of our reforms. My own confidence in what President Butler calls "the findings of mankind" is gone, and the process by which it was lost will become obvious as we proceed. I have no reforms to recommend, except the liberation of Intelligence, which is the first and most essential one. I propose to review by way of introduction some of the new ideas which have been emerging during the past few years in regard to our minds and their operations. Then we shall proceed to the main theme of the book, a sketch of the manner in which our human intelligence appears to have come about. If anyone will follow the story with a fair degree of sympathy and patience he may, by merely putting together well-substantiated facts, many of which he doubtless knows in other connections, hope better to understand the perilous quandary in which mankind is now placed and the ways of escape that offer themselves.

II

II

Good sense is, of all things among men, the most equally distributed; for everyone thinks himself so abundantly provided with it that those even who are the most difficult to satisfy in everything else do not usually desire a larger measure of this quality than they already possess.—DESCARTES.

We see man to-day, instead of the frank and courageous recognition of his status, the docile attention to his biological history, the determination to let nothing stand in the way of the security and permanence of his future, which alone can establish the safety and happiness of the race, substituting blind confidence in his destiny, unclouded faith in the essentially respectful attitude of the universe toward his moral code, and a belief no less firm that his traditions and laws and institutions necessarily contain permanent qualities of reality.
—WILLIAM TROTTER.

3. ON VARIOUS KINDS OF THINKING

THE truest and most profound observations on Intelligence have in the past been made by the poets and, in recent times, by story-writers. They have been keen observers and recorders and reckoned freely with the emotions and sentiments. Most philosophers, on the other hand, have exhibited a grotesque ignorance of man's life and have built up systems that are elaborate and imposing, but quite unrelated to actual human affairs. They have almost consistently neglected the actual process of thought and have set the mind off as something apart to be studied by itself. *But no such mind, exempt from bodily processes, animal impulses, savage traditions, infantile impressions, conventional reactions, and traditional knowledge, ever existed,* even in the case of the most abstract of metaphysicians. Kant entitled his great work *A Critique of Pure Reason.* But to the modern student of mind pure reason seems as mythical as the pure gold, transparent as glass, with which the celestial city is paved.

Formerly philosophers thought of mind as having to do exclusively with conscious thought. It was that within man which perceived, remembered, judged, reasoned, understood, believed, willed. But of late it has been shown that we are unaware of a great part of what we perceive, remember, will, and infer; and that a great part of the thinking of which we are aware is determined by that of which we are not conscious. It has indeed been demonstrated that our unconscious psychic life far outruns our conscious. This seems perfectly natural to anyone who considers the following facts:

The sharp distinction between the mind and the body is, as we shall find, a very ancient and spontaneous uncritical savage prepossession. What we think of as "mind" is so intimately associated with what we call "body" that we are coming to realize that the one cannot be understood without the other. Every thought reverberates through the body, and, on the other hand, alterations in our physical condition affect our whole attitude of mind. The insufficient elimination of the foul and decaying products of digestion may plunge us into deep melancholy, whereas a few whiffs of nitrous monoxide may exalt us to the seventh heaven of supernal knowledge and godlike complacency. And *vice versa*, a sudden word or thought may cause our heart to jump, check our breathing, or make our knees as water. There is a whole new literature growing up which studies the effects of our bodily secretions and our muscular tensions and their relation to our emotions and our thinking.

Then there are hidden impulses and desires and secret longings of which we can only with the greatest difficulty take account. They influence our conscious thought in the most bewildering fashion. Many of these unconscious influences appear to originate in our very early years. The older philosophers seem to have forgotten that even they were infants and children at their most impressionable age and never could by any possibility get over it.

The term "unconscious," now so familiar to all readers of modern works on psychology, gives offense to some adherents of the past. There should, however, be no special mystery about it. It is not a new animistic abstraction, but simply a collective word to include all the physiological changes which escape our notice, all the forgotten experiences and impressions of the past which continue to influence our desires and reflections and conduct, even if we cannot remember them. What we can remember at any time is indeed an infinitesimal part of what has happened to us. We could not remember anything unless we forgot almost everything. As Bergson says, the brain is the organ of forgetfulness as well as of memory. Moreover, we tend, of course, to become oblivious to things to which we are thoroughly accustomed, for habit blinds us to their existence. So the forgotten and the habitual make up a great part of the so-called "unconscious."

If we are ever to understand man, his conduct and reasoning, and if we aspire to learn to guide his life and his relations with his fellows more happily than heretofore, we cannot neglect the great discoveries briefly noted above. We must reconcile ourselves to novel and revolutionary conceptions of the mind, for it is clear that the older philosophers, whose works still determine our current views, had a very superficial notion of the subject with which they dealt. But for our purposes, with due regard to what has just been said and to much that has necessarily been left unsaid (and with the indulgence of those who will at first be inclined to dissent), *we shall consider mind chiefly as conscious knowledge and intelligence, as what we know and our attitude toward it—our disposition to increase our information, classify it, criticize it, and apply it.*

We do not think enough about thinking, and much of our confusion is the result of current illusions in regard to it. Let us forget for the moment any impressions we may have derived from the philosophers, and see what seems to happen in ourselves. The first thing that we notice is that our thought moves with such incredible rapidity that it is almost impossible to arrest any specimen of it long enough to have a look at it. When we are offered a penny for our thoughts we always find that we have recently had so many things in mind that we can easily make a selection which will not compromise us too nakedly. On inspection we shall find that even if we are not downright ashamed of a great part of our spontaneous thinking it is far too intimate, personal, ignoble or trivial to permit us to reveal more than a small part of it. I believe this must be true of everyone. We do not, of course, know what goes on in other people's heads. They tell us very little and we tell them very little. The spigot of speech, rarely fully opened, could never emit more than driblets of the ever renewed hogshead of thought — *noch grösser wie's Heidelberger Fass*. We find it hard to believe that other people's thoughts are as silly as our own, but they probably are.

We all appear to ourselves to be thinking all the time during our waking hours, and most of us are aware that we go on thinking while we are asleep, even more foolishly than when awake. When uninterrupted by some practical issue we are engaged in what is now known as a _reverie_. This is our spontaneous and favorite kind of thinking. We allow our ideas to take their own course and this course is determined by our hopes and fears, our spontaneous desires, their fulfillment or frustration; by our likes and dislikes, our loves and hates and resentments. There is nothing else anything like so interesting to ourselves as ourselves. All thought that is not more or less laboriously controlled and directed will inevitably circle about the beloved Ego. It is amusing and pathetic to observe this tendency in ourselves and in others. We learn politely and generously to overlook this truth, but if we dare to think of it, it blazes forth like the noontide sun.

The reverie or "free association of ideas" has of late become the subject of scientific research. While investigators are not yet agreed on the results, or at least on the proper interpretation to be given to them, there can be no doubt that our reveries form the chief index to our fundamental character. They

ON VARIOUS KINDS OF THINKING

are a reflection of our nature as modified by often hidden and forgotten experiences. We need not go into the matter further here, for it is only necessary to observe that the reverie is at all times a potent and in many cases an omnipotent rival to every other kind of thinking. It doubtless influences all our speculations in its persistent tendency to self-magnification and self-justification, which are its chief preoccupations, but it is the last thing to make directly or indirectly for honest increase of knowledge.[1] Philosophers usually talk as if such thinking did not exist or were in some way negligible. This is what makes their speculations so unreal and often worthless.

The reverie, as any of us can see for himself, is frequently broken and interrupted by the necessity of a second kind of thinking. We have to make practical decisions. Shall

---

[1] The poet-clergyman, John Donne, who lived in the time of James I, has given a beautifully honest picture of the doings of a saint's mind: "I throw myself down in my chamber and call in and invite God and His angels thither, and when they are there I neglect God and His angels for the noise of a fly, for the rattling of a coach, for the whining of a door. I talk on in the same posture of praying, eyes lifted up, knees bowed down, as though I prayed to God, and if God or His angels should ask me when I thought last of God in that prayer I cannot tell. Sometimes I find that I had forgot what I was about, but when I began to forget it I cannot tell. A memory of yesterday's pleasures, a fear of to-morrow's dangers, a straw under my knee, a noise in mine ear, a light in mine eye, an anything, a nothing, a fancy, a chimera in my brain troubles me in my prayer."
—Quoted by ROBERT LYND, *The Art of Letters*, pp. 46–47.

we write a letter or no? Shall we take the subway or a bus? Shall we have dinner at seven or half past? Shall we buy U. S. Rubber or a Liberty Bond? <u>Decisions are easily distinguishable from the free flow of the reverie.</u> Sometimes they demand a good deal of careful pondering and the recollection of pertinent facts; often, however, they are made impulsively. They are a more difficult and laborious thing than the reverie, and we resent having to "make up our mind" when we are tired, or absorbed in a congenial reverie. Weighing a decision, it should be noted, does not necessarily add anything to our knowledge, although we may, of course, seek further information before making it.

4. Rationalizing

A third kind of thinking is stimulated when anyone questions our belief and opinions. We sometimes find ourselves changing our minds without any resistance or heavy emotion, but if we are told that we are wrong we resent the imputation and harden our hearts. We are incredibly heedless in the formation of our beliefs, but find ourselves filled with an illicit passion for them when anyone proposes to rob us of their companionship. It is obviously not the ideas themselves that are dear to us, but our self-esteem, which is threatened. We are by nature stubbornly pledged to defend our own from attack, whether it be our person, our family, our property, or our opinion. A United States Senator once remarked to a friend of mine that God Almighty could not make him change his mind on our Latin-America policy. We may surrender, but rarely confess ourselves vanquished. In the intellectual world at least peace is without victory.

Few of us take the pains to study the origin of our cherished convictions; indeed, we have a natural repugnance to so doing. We like to continue to believe what we have been accustomed to accept as true, and the resentment aroused when doubt is cast upon any of our assumptions leads us to seek every manner of excuse for clinging to them. *The result is that most of our so-called reasoning consists in finding arguments for going on believing as we already do.*

I remember years ago attending a public dinner to which the Governor of the state was bidden. The chairman explained that His Excellency could not be present for certain "good" reasons; what the "real" reasons were the presiding officer said he would leave us to conjecture. This distinction between "good" and "real" reasons is one of the most clarifying and essential in the whole realm of thought. We can readily give what seem to us "good" reasons for being a Catholic or a Mason, a Republican or a Democrat, an adherent or opponent of the League of Nations. But the "real" reasons are usually on quite a different plane. Of course the importance of this distinction is popularly, if somewhat obscurely, recognized. The Baptist missionary is ready enough to see that the Buddhist is not such because his doctrines would bear careful inspection, but because he happened to be born in a Buddhist family in Tokio. But it would be treason to his faith to acknowledge that his own partiality for certain doctrines is due to the fact that his mother was a member of the First Baptist church of Oak Ridge. A savage can give all sorts of reasons for his belief that it is dangerous to step on a man's shadow, and a newspaper editor can advance plenty of arguments against the Bolsheviki. But neither of them may realize why he happens to be defending his particular opinion.

The "real" reasons for our beliefs are concealed from ourselves as well as from others. As we grow up we simply adopt the ideas presented to us in regard to such matters as religion, family relations, property, business, our country, and the state. We unconsciously absorb them from our environment. They are persistently whispered in our ear by the group in which we happen to live. Moreover, as Mr. Trotter has pointed out, these judgments, being the product of suggestion and not of reasoning, have the quality of perfect obviousness, so that to question them

... is to the believer to carry skepticism to an insane degree, and will be met by contempt, disapproval, or condemnation, according to the nature of the belief in question. When, therefore, we find ourselves entertaining an opinion about the basis of which there is a quality of feeling which tells us that to inquire into it would be absurd, obviously unnecessary, unprofitable, undesirable, bad form, or wicked, we may know that that opinion is a nonrational one, and probably, therefore, founded upon inadequate evidence.[1]

Opinions, on the other hand, which are the result of experience or of honest reasoning do not have this quality of "primary certitude." I remember when as a youth I heard a group of business men discussing the question of the immortality of the soul, I was outraged by the sentiment of doubt expressed by one of the party. As I look back now I see that I had at the time no interest in the matter, and certainly no least argument to urge in favor of the belief in which I had been reared. But

[1] *Instincts of the Herd,* p. 44.

neither my personal indifference to the issue, nor the fact that I had previously given it no attention, served to prevent an angry resentment when I heard *my* ideas questioned.

This spontaneous and loyal support of our preconceptions—this process of finding "good" reasons to justify our routine beliefs—is known to modern psychologists as "rationalizing"—clearly only a new name for a very ancient thing. Our "good" reasons ordinarily have no value in promoting honest enlightenment, because, no matter how solemnly they may be marshaled, they are at bottom the result of personal preference or prejudice, and not of an honest desire to seek or accept new knowledge.

In our reveries we are frequently engaged in self-justification, for we cannot bear to think ourselves wrong, and yet have constant illustrations of our weaknesses and mistakes. So we spend much time finding fault with circumstances and the conduct of others, and shifting on to them with great ingenuity the onus of our own failures and disappointments. *Rationalizing is the self-exculpation which occurs when we feel ourselves, or our group, accused of misapprehension or error.*

The little word *my* is the most important one in all human affairs, and properly to reckon with it is the beginning of wisdom. It has the same force whether it is *my* dinner, *my* dog, and *my* house, or *my* faith, *my* country, and *my* God. We not only resent the imputation that our watch is wrong, or our car shabby, but that our conception of the canals of Mars, of the pronunciation of "Epictetus," of the medicinal value of salicine, or the date of Sargon I, are subject to revision.

Philosophers, scholars, and men of science exhibit a common sensitiveness in all decisions in which their *amour propre* is involved. Thousands of argumentative works have been written to vent a grudge. However stately their reasoning, it may be nothing but rationalizing, stimulated by the most commonplace of all motives. A history of philosophy and theology could be written in terms of grouches, wounded pride, and aversions, and it would be far more instructive than the usual treatments of these themes. Sometimes, under Providence, the lowly impulse of resentment leads to great achievements. Milton wrote his treatise on divorce as a result of his troubles with his seventeen-year-old wife, and when he was accused of being the leading spirit in a new sect, the Divorcers, he wrote his noble *Areopagitica* to prove his right to say what he thought fit, and incidentally to establish the advantage of a free press in the promotion of Truth.

All mankind, high and low, thinks in all the ways which have been described. The reverie goes on all the time not only in the mind of the mill hand and the Broadway flapper, but equally in weighty judges and godly bishops. It has gone on in all the philosophers, scientists, poets, and theologians that have ever lived. Aristotle's most abstruse speculations were doubtless tempered by highly irrelevant reflections. He is reported to have had very thin legs and small eyes, for which he doubtless had to find excuses, and he was wont to indulge in very conspicuous dress and rings and was accustomed to arrange his hair carefully.[1] Diogenes the Cynic exhibited the impudence of a touchy soul. His tub was his distinction. Tennyson in beginning his "Maud" could not forget his chagrin over losing his patrimony years before as the result of an unhappy investment in the Patent Decorative Carving Company. These facts are not recalled here as a gratuitous disparagement of the truly great, but to insure a full realization of the tremendous competition which all really ex-

---
[1] Diogenes Lærtius, book v.

acting thought has to face, even in the minds of the most highly endowed mortals.

And now the astonishing and perturbing suspicion emerges that perhaps almost all that had passed for social science, political economy, politics, and ethics in the past may be brushed aside by future generations as mainly rationalizing. John Dewey has already reached this conclusion in regard to philosophy.[1] Veblen[2] and other writers have revealed the various unperceived presuppositions of the traditional political economy, and now comes an Italian sociologist, Vilfredo Pareto, who, in his huge treatise on general sociology, devotes hundreds of pages to substantiating a similar thesis affecting all the social sciences.[3] This conclusion may be ranked by students of a hundred years hence as one of the several great discoveries of our age. It is by no means fully worked out, and it is so opposed to nature that it will be very slowly accepted by the great mass of those who consider themselves thoughtful. As a historical student

---

[1] *Reconstruction in Philosophy.*

[2] *The Place of Science in Modern Civilization.*

[3] *Traité de Sociologie Générale, passim.* The author's term "*derivations*" seems to be his precise way of expressing what we have called the "good" reasons, and his "*residus*" correspond to the "real" reasons. He well says, "*L'homme éprouve le besoin de raisonner, et en outre d'étendre un voile sur ses instincts et sur ses sentiments*" —hence, rationalization. (P. 788.) His aim is to reduce sociology to the "real" reasons. (P. 791.)

I am personally fully reconciled to this newer view. Indeed, it seems to me inevitable that just as the various sciences of nature were, before the opening of the seventeenth century, largely masses of rationalizations to suit the religious sentiments of the period, so the social sciences have continued even to our own day to be rationalizations of uncritically accepted beliefs and customs.

It will become apparent as we proceed that the fact that an idea is ancient and that it has been widely received is no argument in its favor, but should immediately suggest the necessity of carefully testing it as a probable instance of rationalization.

5. How Creative Thought Transforms the World

This brings us to another kind of thought which can fairly easily be distinguished from the three kinds described above. It has not the usual qualities of the reverie, for it does not hover about our personal complacencies and humiliations. It is not made up of the homely decisions forced upon us by everyday needs, when we review our little stock of existing information, consult our conventional preferences and obligations, and make a choice of action. It is not the defense of our own cherished beliefs and prejudices just because they are our own—mere plausible excuses for remaining of the same mind. On the contrary, it is that peculiar species of thought which leads us to *change* our mind.

It is this kind of thought that has raised man from his pristine, subsavage ignorance and squalor to the degree of knowledge and comfort which he now possesses. On his capacity to continue and greatly extend this kind of thinking depends his chance of groping his way out of the plight in which the most highly civilized peoples of the world now find themselves. In the past this type of thinking has been called Reason. But so many misapprehensions have grown up around the word that some of us have become very suspicious of it. I suggest, therefore, that we substitute a recent name and speak of "creative thought" rather than of Reason. *For this kind of meditation begets knowledge, and knowledge is really creative inasmuch as it makes things look different from what they seemed before and may indeed work for their reconstruction.*

In certain moods some of us realize that we are observing things or making reflections with a seeming disregard of our personal preoccupations. We are not preening or defending ourselves; we are not faced by the necessity of any practical decision, nor are we apologizing for believing this or that. We are just wondering and looking and mayhap seeing what we never perceived before.

Curiosity is as clear and definite as any of our urges. We wonder what is in a sealed telegram or in a letter in which some one else is absorbed, or what is being said in the telephone booth or in low conversation. This inquisitiveness is vastly stimulated by jealousy, suspicion, or any hint that we ourselves are directly or indirectly involved. But there appears to be a fair amount of personal interest in other people's affairs even when they do not concern us except as a mystery to be unraveled or a tale to be told. The reports of a divorce suit will have "news value" for many weeks. They constitute a story, like a novel or play or moving picture. This is not an example of pure curiosity, however, since we readily identify ourselves with others, and their joys and despair then become our own.

We also take note of, or "observe," as Sherlock Holmes says, things which have nothing to do with our personal interests and make no personal appeal either direct or by way of sympathy. This is what Veblen so well calls "idle curiosity." And it is usually idle enough. Some of us when we face the line of people opposite us in a subway train impulsively consider them in detail and engage in rapid inferences and form theories in regard to them. On entering a room there are those who will perceive at a glance the degree of preciousness of the rugs, the character of the pictures, and the personality revealed by the books. But there are many, it would seem, who are so absorbed in their personal reverie or in some definite purpose that they have no bright-eyed energy for idle curiosity. The tendency to miscellaneous observation we come by honestly enough, for we note it in many of our animal relatives.

Veblen, however, uses the term "idle curiosity" somewhat ironically, as is his wont. It is idle only to those who fail to realize that it may be a very rare and indispensable thing from which almost all distinguished human achievement proceeds. Since it may lead to systematic examination and seeking for things hitherto undiscovered. For research is but diligent search which enjoys the high flavor of primitive hunting. Occasionally and fitfully idle curiosity thus leads to creative thought, which alters and broadens our own views and aspirations and may in turn, under highly favorable circumstances, affect the views and lives of others, even for generations to follow. An example or two will make this unique human process clear.

Galileo was a thoughtful youth and doubtless carried on a rich and varied reverie. He had artistic ability and might have turned out to be a musician or painter. When he had dwelt among the monks at Valambrosa he had been tempted to lead the life of a religious. As a boy he busied himself with toy machines and he inherited a fondness for mathematics. All these facts are of record. We may safely assume also that, along with many other subjects of contemplation, the Pisan maidens found a vivid place in his thoughts.

One day when seventeen years old he wandered into the cathedral of his native town. In the midst of his reverie he looked up at the lamps hanging by long chains from the high ceiling of the church. Then something very difficult to explain occurred. He found himself no longer thinking of the building, worshipers, or the services; of his artistic or religious interests; of his reluctance to become a physician as his father wished. He forgot the question of a career and even the *graziosissime donne*. As he watched the swinging lamps he was suddenly wondering if mayhap their oscillations, whether long or short, did

CREATIVE THOUGHT

not occupy the same time. Then he tested this hypothesis by counting his pulse, for that was the only timepiece he had with him.

This observation, however remarkable in itself, was not enough to produce a really creative thought. Others may have noticed the same thing and yet nothing came of it. Most of our observations have no assignable results. Galileo may have seen that the warts on a peasant's face formed a perfect isosceles triangle, or he may have noticed with boyish glee that just as the officiating priest was uttering the solemn words, *ecce agnus Dei*, a fly lit on the end of his nose. To be really creative, ideas have to be worked up and then "put over," so that they become a part of man's social heritage. The highly accurate pendulum clock was one of the later results of Galileo's discovery. He himself was led to reconsider and successfully to refute the old notions of falling bodies. It remained for Newton to prove that the moon was falling, and presumably all the heavenly bodies. This quite upset all the consecrated views of the heavens as managed by angelic engineers. The universality of the laws of gravitation stimulated the attempt to seek other and equally important natural laws and cast grave doubts on the miracles in which mankind had hitherto believed. In short, those who dared to include in their thought the discoveries of Galileo and his successors found themselves in a new earth surrounded by new heavens.

On the 28th of October, 1831, three hundred and fifty years after Galileo had noticed the isochronous vibrations of the lamps, creative thought and its currency had so far increased that Faraday was wondering what would happen if he mounted a disk of copper between the poles of a horseshoe magnet. As the disk revolved an electric current was produced. This would doubtless have seemed the idlest kind of an experiment to the stanch business men of the time, who, it happened, were just then denouncing the child-labor bills in their anxiety to avail themselves to the full of the results of earlier idle curiosity. But should the dynamos and motors which have come into being as the outcome of Faraday's experiment be stopped this evening, the business man of to-day, agitated over labor troubles, might, as he trudged home past lines of "dead" cars, through dark streets to an unlighted house, engage in a little creative thought of his own and perceive that he and his laborers would have no modern factories and mines to quarrel about had it not been for the strange practical effects of the idle curiosity of scientists, inventors, and engineers.

The examples of creative intelligence given above belong to the realm of modern scientific achievement, which furnishes the most striking instances of the effects of scrupulous, objective thinking. But there are, of course, other great realms in which the recording and embodiment of acute observation and insight have wrought themselves into the higher life of man. The great poets and dramatists and our modern story-tellers have found themselves engaged in productive reveries, noting and artistically presenting their discoveries for the delight and instruction of those who have the ability to appreciate them.

The process by which a fresh and original poem or drama comes into being is doubtless analogous to that which originates and elaborates so-called scientific discoveries; but there is clearly a temperamental difference. The genesis and advance of painting, sculpture, and music offer still other problems. We really as yet know shockingly little about these matters, and indeed very few people have the least curiosity about them.[1] Never-

---

[1] Recently a re-examination of creative thought has begun as a result of new knowledge which discredits many of the notions formerly held about "reason." See, for example, *Creative Intelligence*, by a group of American philosophic thinkers; John Dewey, *Essays in*

theless, creative intelligence in its various forms and activities is what makes man. Were it not for its slow, painful, and constantly discouraged operations through the ages man would be no more than a species of primate living on seeds, fruit, roots, and uncooked flesh, and wandering naked through the woods and over the plains like a chimpanzee.

The origin and progress and future promotion of civilization are ill understood and misconceived. These should be made the chief theme of education, but much hard work is necessary before we can reconstruct our ideas of man and his capacities and free ourselves from innumerable persistent misapprehensions. There have been obstructionists in all times, not merely the lethargic masses, but the moralists, the rationalizing theologians, and most of the philosophers, all busily if unconsciously engaged in ratifying existing ignorance and mistakes and discouraging creative thought. Naturally, those who reassure us seem worthy of honor and respect. Equally naturally those who puzzle us with disturbing criticisms and invite us to change our ways are objects of suspicion and readily dis-

Experimental Logic (both pretty hard books); and Veblen, *The Place of Science in Modern Civilization*. Easier than these and very stimulating are Dewey, *Reconstruction in Philosophy*, and Woodworth, *Dynamic Psychology*.

credited. Our personal discontent does not ordinarily extend to any critical questioning of the general situation in which we find ourselves. In every age the prevailing conditions of civilization have appeared quite natural and inevitable to those who grew up in them. The cow asks no questions as to how it happens to have a dry stall and a supply of hay. The kitten laps its warm milk from a china saucer, without knowing anything about porcelain; the dog nestles in the corner of a divan with no sense of obligation to the inventors of upholstery and the manufacturers of down pillows. So we humans accept our breakfasts, our trains and telephones and orchestras and movies, our national Constitution, or moral code and standards of manners, with the simplicity and innocence of a pet rabbit. We have absolutely inexhaustible capacities for appropriating what others do for us with no thought of a "thank you." We do not feel called upon to make any least contribution to the merry game ourselves. Indeed, we are usually quite unaware that a game is being played at all.

We have now examined the various classes of thinking which we can readily observe in ourselves and which we have plenty of reasons to believe go on, and always have been going on, in our fellow-men. We can sometimes get quite pure and sparkling examples of all four kinds, but commonly they are so confused and intermingled in our reverie as not to be readily distinguishable. The reverie is a reflection of our longings, exultations, and complacencies, our fears, suspicions, and disappointments. We are chiefly engaged in struggling to maintain our self-respect and in asserting that supremacy which we all crave and which seems to us our natural prerogative. It is not strange, but rather quite inevitable, that our beliefs about what is true and false, good and bad, right and wrong, should be mixed up with the reverie and be influenced by the same considerations which determine its character and course. We resent criticisms of our views exactly as we do of anything else connected with ourselves. Our notions of life and its ideals seem to us to be *our own* and as such necessarily true and right, to be defended at all costs.

We very rarely consider, however, the process by which we gained our convictions. If we did so, we could hardly fail to see that there was usually little ground for our confidence in them. Here and there, in this department of knowledge or that, some one of us might

CREATIVE THOUGHT

make a fair claim to have taken some trouble to get correct ideas of, let us say, the situation in Russia, the sources of our food supply, the origin of the Constitution, the revision of the tariff, the policy of the Holy Roman Apostolic Church, modern business organization, trade unions, birth control, socialism, the League of Nations, the excess-profits tax, preparedness, advertising in its social bearings; but only a very exceptional person would be entitled to opinions on all of even these few matters. And yet most of us have opinions on all these, and on many other questions of equal importance, of which we may know even less. We feel compelled, as self-respecting persons, to take sides when they come up for discussion. We even surprise ourselves by our omniscience. Without taking thought we see in a flash that it is most righteous and expedient to discourage birth control by legislative enactment, or that one who decries intervention in Mexico is clearly wrong, or that big advertising is essential to big business and that big business is the pride of the land. As godlike beings why should we not rejoice in our omniscience?

It is clear, in any case, that our convictions on important matters are not the result of knowledge or critical thought, nor, it may be added, are they often dictated by supposed self-interest. Most of them are *pure prejudices* in the proper sense of that word. We do not form them ourselves. They are the whisperings of "the voice of the herd." We have in the last analysis no responsibility for them and need assume none. They are not really our own ideas, but those of others no more well informed or inspired than ourselves, who have got them in the same careless and humiliating manner as we. It should be our pride to revise our ideas and not to adhere to what passes for respectable opinion, for such opinion can frequently be shown to be not respectable at all. We should, in view of the considerations that have been mentioned, resent our supine credulity. As an English writer has remarked:

"If we feared the entertaining of an unverifiable opinion with the warmth with which we fear using the wrong implement at the dinner table, if the thought of holding a prejudice disgusted us as does a foul disease, then the dangers of man's suggestibility would be turned into advantages."[1]

The purpose of this essay is to set forth briefly the way in which the notions of the

---

[1] Trotter, *op. cit.*, p. 45. The first part of this little volume is excellent.

herd have been accumulated. This seems to me the best, easiest, and least invidious educational device for cultivating a proper distrust for the older notions on which we still continue to rely.

The "real" reasons, which explain how it is we happen to hold a particular belief, are chiefly historical. Our most important opinions—those, for example, having to do with traditional, religious, and moral convictions, property rights, patriotism, national honor, the state, and indeed all the assumed foundations of society—are, as I have already suggested, rarely the result of reasoned consideration, but of unthinking absorption from the social environment in which we live. Consequently, they have about them a quality of "elemental certitude," and we especially resent doubt or criticism cast upon them. So long, however, as we revere the whisperings of the herd, we are obviously unable to examine them dispassionately and to consider to what extent they are suited to the novel conditions and social exigencies in which we find ourselves to-day.

The "real" reasons for our beliefs, by making clear their origins and history, can do much to dissipate this emotional blockade and rid us of our prejudices and preconceptions. Once this is done and we come critically to examine our traditional beliefs, we may well find some of them sustained by experience and honest reasoning, while others must be revised to meet new conditions and our more extended knowledge. But only after we have undertaken such a critical examination in the light of experience and modern knowledge, freed from any feeling of "primary certitude," can we claim that the "good" are also the "real" reasons for our opinions.

I do not flatter myself that this general show-up of man's thought through the ages will cure myself or others of carelessness in adopting ideas, or of unseemly heat in defending them just because we have adopted them. But if the considerations which I propose to recall are really incorporated into our thinking and are permitted to establish our general outlook on human affairs, they will do much to relieve the imaginary obligation we feel in regard to traditional sentiments and ideals. Few of us are capable of engaging in creative thought, but some of us can at least come to distinguish it from other and inferior kinds of thought and accord to it the esteem that it merits as the greatest treasure of the past and the only hope of the future.

III

III

Nous étions déjà si vieux quand nous sommes nés.
—ANATOLE FRANCE.

Simia quam similis, turpissima bestia, nobis?—ENNIUS.

Tous les hommes se ressemblent si fort qu'il n'y a point de peuple dont les sottises ne nous doivent faire trembler.—FONTENELLE.

The savage is very close to us indeed, both in his physical and mental make-up and in the forms of his social life. Tribal society is virtually delayed civilization, and the savages are a sort of contemporaneous ancestry.
—WILLIAM I. THOMAS.

6. Our Animal Heritage. The Nature of Civilization

THERE are four historical layers underlying the minds of civilized men—the animal mind, the child mind, the savage mind, and the traditional civilized mind. We are all animals and never can cease to be; we were all children at our most impressionable age and can never get over the effects of that; our human ancestors have lived in savagery during practically the whole existence of the race, say five hundred thousand or a million years, and the primitive human mind is ever with us; finally, we are all born into an elaborate civilization, the constant pressure of which we can by no means escape.

Each of these underlying minds has its special sciences and appropriate literatures. The new discipline of animal or comparative psychology deals with the first; genetic and analytical psychology with the second;[1] an-

---

[1] It is impossible to discuss here the results which a really honest study of child psychology promises. The relations of the child to his parents and elders in general and to the highly artificial system of censorship and restraints which they impose in their own interests on his natural impulses must surely have a permanent influence on the notions he continues to have as an adult in regard to his

thropology, ethnology, and comparative religion with the third; and the history of philosophy, science, theology, and literature with the fourth.

We may grow beyond these underlying minds and in the light of new knowledge we may criticize their findings and even persuade ourselves that we have successfully trancended them. But if we are fair with ourselves we shall find that their hold on us is really inexorable. We can only transcend them artificially and precariously and in certain highly favorable conditions. Depression, anger, fear, or ordinary irritation will speedily prove the insecurity of any structure that we manage to rear on our fourfold foundation. Such fundamental and vital preoccupations as religion, love, war, and the chase stir impulses that lie far back in human history and which effectually repudiate the cavilings of ratiocination.

In all our reveries and speculations, even the most exacting, sophisticated, and disillusioned, we have three unsympathetic companions sticking closer than a brother and looking on with jealous impatience — our

---

"superiors" and the institutions and *mores* under which he is called to live. Attempts in later life to gain intellectual freedom can only be successful if one comes to think of the childish origin of a great part of his "real" reasons.

wild apish progenitor, a playful or peevish baby, and a savage. We may at any moment find ourselves overtaken with a warm sense of camaraderie for any or all of these ancient pals of ours, and experience infinite relief in once more disporting ourselves with them as of yore. Some of us have in addition a Greek philosopher or man of letters in us; some a neoplatonic mystic, some a mediæval monk, all of whom have learned to make terms with their older playfellows.

Before retracing the way in which the mind as we now find it in so-called intelligent people has been accumulated, we may take time to try to see what civilization is and why man alone can become civilized. For the mind has expanded *pari passu* with civilization, and without civilization there would, I venture to conjecture, have been no human mind in the commonly accepted sense of that term.

It is now generally conceded by all who have studied the varied evidence and have freed themselves from ancient prejudice that, if we traced back our human lineage far enough we should come to a point where our human ancestors had no civilization and lived a speechless, naked, houseless, fireless, and toolless life, similar to that of the existing primates with which we are zoölogically closely connected.

This is one of the most fully substantiated of historical facts and one which we can never neglect in our attempts to explain man as he now is. We are all descended from the lower animals. We are furthermore still animals with not only an animal body, but with an animal mind. And this animal body and animal mind are the original foundations on which even the most subtle and refined intellectual life must perforce rest.

We are ready to classify certain of our most essential desires as brutish—hunger and thirst, the urgence of sleep, and especially sexual longing. We know of blind animal rage, of striking, biting, scratching, howling, and snarling, of irrational fears and ignominious flight. We share our senses with the higher animals, have eyes and ears, noses and tongues much like theirs; heart, lungs, and other viscera, and four limbs. They have brains which stand them in good stead, although their heads are not so good as ours. But when one speaks of the animal mind he should think of still other resemblances between the brute and man.

All animals learn—even the most humble among them may gain something from experience. All the higher animals exhibit curiosity under certain circumstances, and it is this impulse which underlies all human science.

Moreover, some of the higher animals, especially the apes and monkeys, are much given to fumbling and groping. They are restless, easily bored, and spontaneously experimental. They therefore make discoveries quite unconsciously, and form new and sometimes profitable habits of action. If, by mere fumbling, a monkey, cat, or dog happens on a way to secure food, this remunerative line of conduct will "occur" to the creature when he feels hungry. This is what Thorndike has named learning by "trial and error." It might better be called "fumbling and success," for it is the success that establishes the association. The innate curiosity which man shares with his uncivilized zoölogical relatives is the native impulse that leads to scientific and philosophical speculation, and the original fumbling of a restless ape has become the ordered experimental investigation of modern times. A creature which lacked curiosity and had no tendency to fumble could never have developed civilization and human intelligence.[1]

But why did man alone of all the animals become civilized? The reason is not far to seek, although it has often escaped writers

---

[1] Clarence Day in *Our Simian World* discusses with delightful humor the effects of our underlying simian temperament on the conduct of life.

on the subject. All animals gain a certain wisdom with age and experience, but the experience of one ape does not profit another. Learning among animals below man is *individual*, not *co-operative* and *cumulative*. One dog does not seem to learn from another, nor one ape from another, in spite of the widespread misapprehension in this regard. Many experiments have been patiently tried in recent years and it seems to be pretty well established that the monkey learns by *monkeying*, but that he rarely or never appears to *ape*. He does not learn by imitation, because he does not imitate. There may be minor exceptions, but the fact that apes never, in spite of a bodily equipment nearly human, become in the least degree civilized, would seem to show that the accumulation of knowledge or dexterity through imitation is impossible for them.

Man has the various sense organs of the apes and their extraordinary power of manipulation. To these essentials he adds a brain sufficiently more elaborate than that of the chimpanzee to enable him to do something that the ape cannot do—namely, "see" things clearly enough to form associations through imitation.[1]

---

[1] The word "imitation" is commonly used very loosely. The real question is does an animal, or even man himself, tend to make

We can imagine the manner in which man unwittingly took one of his momentous and unprecedented first steps in civilization. Some restless primeval savage might find himself scraping the bark off a stick with the edge of a stone or shell and finally cutting into the wood and bringing the thing to a point. He might then spy an animal and, quite without reasoning, impulsively make a thrust with the stick and discover that it pierced the creature. If he could hold these various elements in the situation, sharpening the stick and using it, he would have made an invention—a rude spear. A particularly acute bystander might comprehend and imitate the process. If others did so and the habit was established in the tribe so that it became traditional and was transmitted to following generations, the process of civilization would have begun— also the process of human learning, which is noticing distinctions and analyzing situations. This simple process of sharpening a stick would involve the "concepts," as the philosophers say, of a tool and bark and a point and

---

movements or sounds made by their fellow-creatures in their presence? It seems to be made out now that even monkeys are not imitative in that sense and that man himself has no *general* inclination to do over what he sees being done. Pray, if you doubt this, note how many things you see others doing that you have no inclination to imitate! For an admirable summary see Thorndike, E. L., *The Original Nature of Man*, 1913, pp. 108 ff.

an artificial weapon. But ages and ages were to elapse before the botanist would distinguish the various layers which constitute the bark, or successive experimenters come upon the idea of a bayonet to take the place of the spear.

Of late, considerable attention has been given to the question of man's original, uneducated, animal nature; what resources has he as a mere creature independent of any training that results from being brought up in some sort of civilized community? The question is difficult to formulate satisfactorily and still more difficult to answer. But without attempting to list man's supposed natural "instincts" we must assume that civilization is built up on his original propensities and impulses, whatever they may be. These probably remain nearly the same from generation to generation. The idea formerly held that the civilization of our ancestors affects our original nature is almost completely surrendered. *We are all born wholly uncivilized.*

If a group of infants from the "best" families of to-day could be reared by apes they would find themselves with no civilization. How long it would take them and their children to gain what now passes for even a low savage culture it is impossible to say. The whole arduous task would have to be performed anew and it might not take place at all, unless conditions were favorable, for man is not naturally a "progressive" animal. He shares the tendency of all other animal tribes just to pull through and reproduce his kind.

Most of us do not stop to think of the conditions of an animal existence. When we read the descriptions of our nature as given by William James, McDougall, or even Thorndike, with all his reservations, we get a rather impressive idea of our possibilities, not a picture of uncivilized life. When we go camping we think that we are deserting civilization, forgetting the sophisticated guides, and the pack horses laden with the most artificial luxuries, many of which would not have been available even a hundred years ago. We lead the simple life with Swedish matches, Brazilian coffee, Canadian bacon, California canned peaches, magazine rifles, jointed fishing rods, and electric flashlights. We are elaborately clothed and can discuss Bergson's views or D. H. Lawrence's last story. We naïvely imagine we are returning to "primitive" conditions because we are living out of doors or sheltered in a less solid abode than usual, and have to go to the brook for water.

But man's original estate was, as Hobbes reflected, "poor, nasty, brutish, and short."

To live like an animer is to rely upon one's own quite naked equipment and efforts, and not to mind getting wet or cold or scratching one's bare legs in the underbrush. One would have to eat his roots and seeds quite raw, and gnaw a bird as a cat does. To get the feel of uncivilized life, let us recall how savages with the comparatively advanced degree of culture reached by our native Indian tribes may fall to when really hungry. In the journal of the Lewis and Clark expedition there is an account of the killing of a deer by the white men. Hearing of this, the Shoshones raced wildly to the spot where the warm and bloody entrails had been thrown out

> ... and ran tumbling over one another like famished dogs. Each tore away whatever part he could, and instantly began to eat it; some had the liver, some the kidneys, and, in short, no part on which we are accustomed to look with disgust escaped them. One of them who had seized about nine feet of the entrails was chewing at one end, while with his hand he was diligently clearing his way by discharging the contents at the other.

Another striking example of simple animal procedure is given in the same journal:

> One of the women, who had been leading two of our pack horses, halted at a rivulet about a mile behind and sent on the two horses by a female friend. On inquiring of Cameahwait the cause of her detention,

he answered, with great apparent unconcern, that she had just stopped to lie in, but would soon overtake us. In fact, we were astonished to see her in about an hour's time come on with her new-born infant, and pass us on her way to the camp, seemingly in perfect health.

This is the simple life and it was the life of our ancestors before civilization began. It had been the best kind of life possible in all the preceding æons of the world's history. Without civilization it would be the existence to which all human beings now on the earth would forthwith revert. It is man's starting point.[1]

But what about the mind? What was going on in the heads of our untutored forbears?

---

[1] "If the earth were struck by one of Mr. Wells's comets, and if, in consequence, every human being now alive were to lose all the knowledge and habits which he had acquired from preceding generations (though retaining unchanged all his own powers of invention and memory and habituation) nine tenths of the inhabitants of London or New York would be dead in a month, and 99 per cent of the remaining tenth would be dead in six months. They would have no language to express their thoughts, and no thoughts but vague reverie. They could not read notices, or drive motors or horses. They would wander about, led by the inarticulate cries of a few naturally dominant individuals, drowning themselves, as thirst came on, in hundreds at the riverside landing places, looting those shops where the smell of decaying food attracted them, and perhaps at the end stumbling on the expedient of cannibalism. Even in the country districts men could not invent, in time to preserve their lives, methods of growing food, or taming animals, or making fire, or so clothing themselves as to endure a Northern winter."—GRAHAM WALLAS, *Our Social Heritage*, p. 16. Only the very lowest of savages might possibly pull through if culture should disappear.

We are apt to fall into the error of supposing that because they had human brains they must have had somewhat the same kinds of ideas and made the same kind of judgments that we do. Even distinguished philosophers like Descartes and Rousseau made this mistake. This assumption will not stand inspection. To reach back in imagination to the really primitive mind we should of course have to deduct at the start all the knowledge and all the discriminations and classifications that have grown up as a result of our education and our immersion from infancy in a highly artificial environment. Then we must recollect that our primitive ancestor had no words with which to name and tell about things. He was speechless. His fellows knew no more than he did. Each one learned during his lifetime according to his capacity, but no instruction in our sense of the word was possible. What he saw and heard was not what we should have called seeing and hearing. He responded to situations in a blind and impulsive manner, with no clear idea of them. In short, he must have *thought* much as a wolf or bear does, just as he *lived* much like them.

We must be on our guard against accepting the prevalent notions of even the animal intellect. An owl may look quite as wise as a judge. A monkey, canary, or collie has bright eyes and seems far more alert than most of the people we see on the street car. A squirrel in the park appears to be looking at us much as we look at him. But he cannot be seeing the same things that we do. We can be scarcely more to him than a vague suggestion of peanuts. And even the peanut has little of the meaning for him that it has for us. A dog perceives a motor-car and may be induced to ride in it, but his idea of it would not differ from that of an ancient carryall, except, mayhap, in an appreciative distinction between the odor of gasoline and that of the stable. Only in times of sickness, drunkenness, or great excitement can we get some hint in ourselves of the impulsive responses in animals free from human sophistication and analysis.

Locke thought that we first got simple ideas and then combined them into more complex conceptions and finally into generalizations or abstract ideas. But this is not the way that man's knowledge arose. He started with mere impressions of general situations, and gradually by his ability to handle things he came upon distinctions, which in time he made clearer by attaching names to them.

We keep repeating this process when we

learn about anything. The typewriter is at first a mere mass impression, and only gradually and imperfectly do most of us distinguish certain of its parts; only the men who made it are likely to realize its full complexity by noting and assigning names to all the levers, wheels, gears, bearings, controls, and adjustments. John Stuart Mill thought that the chief function of the mind was making inferences. But making distinctions is equally fundamental—seeing that there are really many things where only one was at first apparent. This process of analysis has been man's supreme accomplishment. This is what has made his mind grow.

The human mind has then been built up through hundreds of thousands of years by gradual accretions and laborious accumulations. Man started at a cultural zero and had to find out everything for himself; or rather a very small number of peculiarly restless and adventurous spirits did the work. The great mass of humanity has never had anything to do with the increase of intelligence except to act as its medium of transfusion and perpetuation. Creative intelligence is confined to the very few, but the many can thoughtlessly avail themselves of the more obvious achievements of those who are exceptionally highly endowed.

Even an ape will fit himself into a civilized environment. A chimpanzee can be taught to relish bicycles, roller skates, and cigarettes which he could never have devised, cannot understand, and could not reproduce. Even so with mankind. Most of us could not have devised, do not understand, and consquently could not reproduce any of the everyday conveniences and luxuries which surround us. Few of us could make an electric light, or write a good novel to read by it, or paint a picture for it to shine upon.

Professor Giddings has recently asked the question, Why has there been any history?[1] Why, indeed, considering that the "good" and "respectable" is usually synonymous with the ancient routine, and the old have always been there to repress the young? Such heavy words of approval as "venerable," "sanctified," and "revered" all suggest great age rather than fresh discoveries. As it was in the beginning, is now and ever shall be, is our protest against being disturbed, forced to think or to change our habits. So history, *namely change*, has been mainly due to a small number of "seers," —really gropers and monkeyers—whose native curiosity outran that of their fellows and

---
[1] "A Theory of History," *Political Science Quarterly*, December, 1920. He attributes history to the adventurers.

led them to escape here and there from the sanctified blindness of their time.

The seer is simply an example of a *variation* biologically, such as occurs in all species of living things, both animal and vegetable. But the unusually large roses in our gardens, the swifter horses of the herd, and the cleverer wolf in the pack have no means of influencing their fellows as a result of their peculiar superiority. Their offspring has some chance of sharing to some degree this pre-eminence, but otherwise things will go on as before. Whereas the singular variation represented by a St. Francis, a Dante, a Voltaire, or a Darwin may permanently, and for ages to follow change somewhat the character and ambitions of innumerable inferior members of the species who could by no possibility have originated anything for themselves, but who can, nevertheless, suffer some modification as a result of the teachings of others. This illustrates the magical and unique workings of culture and creative intelligence in mankind.[1]

---

[1] Count Korzybski in his *Manhood of Humanity* is so impressed by the uniqueness and undreamed possibilities of human civilization and man's "time-binding" capacity that he declares that it is a gross and misleading error to regard man as an animal at all. Yet he is forced sadly to confess that man continues all too often to operate on an animal or "space-binding" plan of life. His aim and outlook are, however, essentially the same as those of the present writer. His method of approach will appeal especially to those who

We have no means of knowing when or where the first contribution to civilization was made, and with it a start on the arduous building of the mind. There is some reason to think that the men who first transcended the animal mind were of inferior mental capacity to our own, but even if man, emerging from his animal estate, had had on the average quite as good a brain as those with which we are now familiar, I suspect that the extraordinarily slow and hazardous process of accumulating modern civilization would not have been greatly shortened. Mankind is lethargic, easily pledged to routine, timid, suspicious of innovation. That is his nature. He is only artificially, partially, and very recently "progressive." He has spent almost his whole existence as a savage hunter, and in that state of ignorance he illustrated on a magnificent scale all the inherent weaknesses of the human mind.

7. Our Savage Mind

Should we arrange our present beliefs and opinions on the basis of their age, we should find that some of them were very, very old,

---

are wont to deal with affairs in the spirit of the mathematician and engineer. He is quite right in thinking that man has hitherto had little conception of his peculiar prerogatives and unlimited opportunities for betterment.

going back to primitive man; others were derived from the Greeks; many more of them would prove to come directly from the Middle Ages; while certain others in our stock were unknown until natural science began to develop in a new form about three hundred years ago. The idea that man has a soul or double which survives the death of the body is very ancient indeed and is accepted by most savages. Such confidence as we have in the liberal arts, metaphysics, and formal logic goes back to the Greek thinkers; our religious ideas and our standards of sexual conduct are predominantly mediæval in their presuppositions; our notions of electricity and disease germs are, of course, recent in origin, the result of painful and prolonged reasearch which involved the rejection of a vast number of older notions sanctioned by immemorial acceptance.

In general, those ideas which are still almost universally accepted in regard to man's nature, his proper conduct, and his relations to God and his fellows are far more ancient and far less critical than those which have to do with the movement of the stars, the stratification of the rocks and the life of plants and animals.

Nothing is more essential in our attempt to escape from the bondage of consecrated ideas than to get a vivid notion of

OUR SAVAGE MIND

human achievement in its proper historical perspective. In order to do this let us imagine the whole gradual and laborious attainments of mankind compressed into the compass of a single lifetime. Let us assume that a single generation of men have in fifty years managed to accumulate all that now passes for civilization. They would have to start, as all individuals do, absolutely uncivilized, and their task would be to recapitulate what has occupied the race for, let us guess, at least five hundred thousand years. Each year in the life of a generation would therefore correspond to ten thousand years in the progress of the race.

On this scale it would require forty-nine years to reach a point of intelligence which would enable our self-taught generation to give up their ancient and inveterate habits of wandering hunters and settle down here and there to till the ground, harvest their crops, domesticate animals, and weave their rough garments. Six months later, or half through the fiftieth year, some of them, in a particularly favorable situation, would have invented writing and thus established a new and wonderful means of spreading and perpetuating civilization. Three months later another group would have carried literature, art, and philosophy to a high degree of refinement and set standards for the succeeding weeks. For two months our generation would have been living under the blessings of Christianity; the printing press would be but a fortnight old and they would not have had the steam engine for quite a week. For two or three days they would have been hastening about the globe in steamships and railroad trains, and only yesterday would they have come upon the magical possibilities of electricity. Within the last few hours they would have learned to sail in the air and beneath the waters, and have forthwith applied their newest discoveries to the prosecution of a magnificent war on the scale befitting their high ideals and new resources. This is not so strange, for only a week ago they were burning and burying alive those who differed from the ruling party in regard to salvation, eviscerating in public those who had new ideas of government, and hanging old women who were accused of traffic with the devil. All of them had been no better than vagrant savages a year before. Their fuller knowledge was altogether too recent to have gone very deep, and they had many institutions and many leaders dedicated to the perpetuation of outworn notions which would otherwise have disappeared. Until recently changes had taken place so slowly and so insensibly that only a very few persons could be expected to realize that not a few of the beliefs that were accepted as eternal verities were due to the inevitable misunderstandings of a savage.

In speaking of the "savage" or "primitive mind," we are, of course, using a very clumsy expression. We shall employ the term, nevertheless, to indicate the characteristics of the human mind when there was as yet no writing, no organized industry or mechanical arts, no money, no important specialization of function except between the sexes, no settled life in large communities. The period so described covers all but about five or six thousand of the half million to a million years that man has existed on the earth.

There are no chronicles to tell us the story of those long centuries. Some inferences can be made from the increasing artfulness and variety of the flint weapons and tools which we find. But the stone weapons which have come down to us, even in their crudest forms (eoliths), are very far from representing the earliest achievements of man in the accumulation of culture. Those dim, remote cycles must have been full of great, but inconspicuous, originators who laid the foundations of civilization in discoveries and achievements so long taken for granted that we do not realize that they ever had to be made at all.

Since man is descended from less highly endowed animals, there must have been a time when the man-animal was in a state of animal ignorance. He started with no more than an ape is able to know. He had to learn everything for himself, as he had no one to teach him the tricks that apes and children can be taught by sophisticated human beings. He was necessarily self-taught, and began, as we have seen, in a state of ignorance beyond anything we can readily conceive. He lived naked and speechless in the woods, or wandered over the plains without artificial shelter or any way of cooking his food. He subsisted on raw fruit, berries, roots, insects, and such animals as he could strike down or pick up dead. His mind must have corresponded with his brutish state. He must at the first have learned just as his animal relatives learn—by fumbling and by forming accidental associations. He had impulses and such sagacity as he individually derived from experience, but no heritage of knowledge accumulated by the group and transmitted by education. This heritage had to be constructed on man's potentialities.

Of mankind in this extremely primitive

condition we have no traces. There could indeed be no traces. All savages of the present day or of whom we have any record represent a relatively highly developed traditional culture, with elaborate languages, myths, and well-established artificial customs, which it probably took hundreds of thousands of years to accumulate. Man in "a state of nature" is only a presupposition, but a presupposition which is forced upon us by compelling evidence, conjectural and inferential though it is.

On a geological time scale we are still close to savagery, and it is inevitable that the ideas and customs and sentiments of savagery should have become so ingrained that they may have actually affected man's nature by natural selection through the survival of those who most completely adjusted themselves to the uncritical culture which prevailed. But in any case it is certain, as many anthropologists have pointed out, that customs, savage ideas, and primitive sentiments have continued to form an important part of our own culture down even to the present day. We are met thus with the necessity of reckoning with this inveterate element in our present thought and customs. Much of the data that we have regarding primitive man has been accumulated in recent times, for the most part as a result of the study of simple peoples. These differ greatly in their habits and myths, but some salient common traits emerge which cast light on the spontaneous workings of the human mind when unaffected by the sophistications of a highly elaborate civilization.

At the start man had to distinguish himself from the group to which he belonged and say, "I am I." This is not an idea given by nature.[1] There are evidences that the earlier religious notions were not based on individuality, but rather on the "virtue" which objects had—that is, their potency to do things. Only later did the animistic belief in the personalities of men, animals, and the forces of nature appear. When man discovered his own individuality he spontaneously ascribed the same type of individuality and purpose to animals and plants, to the wind and the thunder.

This exhibits one of the most noxious tendencies of the mind—namely, personification. It is one of the most virulent enemies of clear thinking. We speak of the Spirit of the

---

[1] In the beginning, too, man did not know how children came about, for it was not easy to connect a common impulsive act with the event of birth so far removed in time. The tales told to children still are reminiscences of the mythical explanations which our savage ancestors advanced to explain the arrival of the infant. Consequently, all popular theories of the origin of marriage and the family based on the assumption of conscious paternity are outlawed.

Reformation or the Spirit of Revolt or the Spirit of Disorder and Anarchy. The papers tell us that, "Berlin says," "London says," "Uncle Sam so decides," "John Bull is disgruntled." Now, whether or no there are such things as spirits, Berlin and London have no souls, and Uncle Sam is as mythical as the great god Pan. Sometimes this regression to the savage is harmless, but when a newspaper states that "Germany is as militaristic as ever," on the ground that some insolent Prussian lieutenant says that German armies will occupy Paris within five years, we have an example of animism which in a society farther removed from savagery than ours might be deemed a high crime and misdemeanor. Chemists and physicians have given up talking of spirits, but in discussing social and economic questions we are still victimized by the primitive animistic tendencies of the mind.

<u>The dream has had a great influence in the building up of the mind</u>. Our ideas, especially our religious beliefs, would have had quite another history had men been dreamless. For it was not merely his shadow and his reflection in the water that led man to imagine souls and doubles, but pre-eminently the visions of the night. As his body lay quiet in sleep he found himself wandering in distant places.

Sometimes he was visited by the dead. So it was clear that the body had an inhabitant who was not necessarily bound to it, who could desert it from time to time during life, and who continued to exist and interest itself in human affairs after death.

Whole civilizations and religions and vast theological speculations have been dominated by this savage inference. It is true that in very recent times, since Plato, let us say, other reasons have been urged for believing in the soul and its immortality, but the idea appears to have got its firm footing in savage logic. It is a primitive inference, however it may later have been revised, rationalized, and ennobled.

The taboo—the forbidden thing—of savage life is another thing very elementary in man's make-up. He had tendencies to fall into habits and establish inhibitions for reasons that he either did not discover or easily forgot. These became fixed and sacred to him and any departure from them filled him with dread. Sometimes the prohibition might have some reasonable justification, sometimes it might seem wholly absurd and even a great nuisance, but that made no difference in its binding force. For example, pork was taboo among the ancient Hebrews—no one can say why, but none of the modern justifications for abstaining from that particular kind of meat would have counted in early Jewish times. It is not improbable that it was the original veneration for the boar and not an abhorrence of him that led to the prohibition.

The modern "principle" is too often only a new form of the ancient taboo, rather than an enlightened rule of conduct. The person who justifies himself by saying that he holds certain beliefs, or acts in a certain manner "on principle," and yet refuses to examine the basis and expediency of his principle, introduces into his thinking and conduct an irrational, mystical element similar to that which characterized savage prohibitions. Principles unintelligently urged make a great deal of trouble in the free consideration of social readjustment, for they are frequently as recalcitrant and obscurantist as the primitive taboo, and are really scarcely more than an excuse for refusing to reconsider one's convictions and conduct. The psychological conditions lying back of both taboo and this sort of principle are essentially the same.

We find in savage thought a sort of intensified and generalized taboo in the classification of things as clean and unclean and in the conceptions of the sacred. These are really expressions of profound and persistent traits in the uncritical mind and can only be overcome by carefully cultivated criticism. They are the result of our natural timidity and the constant dread lest we find ourselves treading on holy (*i. e.*, dangerous) ground.[1] When they are intrenched in the mind we cannot expect to think freely and fairly, for they effectually stop argument. If a thing is held to be sacred it is the center of what may be called a defense complex, and a reasonable consideration of the merits of the case will not be tolerated. When an issue is declared to be a "moral" one—for example, the prohibition of strong drink—an emotional state is implied which makes reasonable compromise and adjustment impossible; for "moral" is a word on somewhat the same plane as "sacred," and has much the same qualities and similar effects on thinking. In dealing with the relations of the sexes the terms "pure" and "impure" introduce mystic and irrational moods alien to clear analysis and reasonable readjustments.

Those who have studied the characteristics of savage life are always struck by its deadly conservatism, its needless restraints on the freedom of the individual, and its hopeless

---

[1] Lucretius warns the reader not to be deterred from considering the evils wrought by religion by the fear of treading on "the unholy grounds of reason and in the path of sin."—*De Rer. Nat.* i, 80 ff.

routine. Man, like plants and animals in general, tends to go on from generation to generation, living as nearly as may be the life of his forbears. Changes have to be forced upon him by hard experience, and he is ever prone to find excuses for slipping back into older habits, for these are likely to be simpler, less critical, more spontaneous—more closely akin, in short, to his animal and primitive promptings. One who prides himself to-day on his conservatism, on the ground that man is naturally an anarchic and disorderly creature who is held in check by the far-seeing Tory, is almost exactly reversing the truth. Mankind is conservative by nature and readily generates restraints on himself and obstacles to change which have served to keep him in a state of savagery during almost his whole existence on the earth, and which still perpetuate all sorts of primitive barbarism in modern society. The conservative "on principle" is therefore a most unmistakably primitive person in his attitude. His only advance beyond the savage mood lies in the specious reasons he is able to advance for remaining of the same mind. What we vaguely call a "radical" is a very recent product due to altogether exceptional and unprecedented circumstances.

IV

IV

Thereupon one of the Egyptian priests, who was of a very great age, said: O Solon, Solon, you Hellenes are but children, and there was never an old man who was a Hellene. Solon in return asked him what he meant. I mean to say, he replied, that in mind you are all young; there is no old opinion handed down among you by ancient tradition; nor any science which is hoary with age.—PLATO's *Timæus*, 22 (Jowett's translation).

The truth is that we are far more likely to underrate the originality of the Greeks than to exaggerate it, and we do not always remember the very short time they took to lay down the lines scientific inquiry has followed ever since.—JOHN BURNET.

8. Beginning of Critical Thinking

THE Egyptians were the first people, so far as we know, who invented a highly artificial method of writing, about five thousand years ago, and began to devise new arts beyond those of their barbarous predecessors. They developed painting and architecture, navigation, and various ingenious industries; they worked in glass and enamels and began the use of copper, and so introduced metal into human affairs. But in spite of their extraordinary advance in practical, matter-of-fact knowledge they remained very primitive in their beliefs. The same may be said of the peoples of Mesopotamia and of the western Asiatic nations in general—just as in our own day the practical arts have got a long start compared with the revision of beliefs in regard to man and the gods. The peculiar opinions of the Egyptians do not enter directly into our intellectual heritage, but some of the fundamental religious ideas which developed in western Asia have, through the veneration for the Hebrew Scriptures, become part and parcel of our ways of thinking.

To the Greeks, however, we are intellectually under heavy obligation. The literature of the Greeks, in such fragments as escaped destruction, was destined, along with the Hebrew Scriptures, to exercise an incalculable influence in the formation of our modern civilized minds. These two dominating literary heritages originated about the same time—day before yesterday—viewed in the perspective of our race's history. Previous to the Greek civilization books had played no great part in the development, dissemination, and transmission of culture from generation to generation. Now they were to become a cardinal force in advancing and retarding the mind's expansion.

It required about a thousand years for the Greek shepherds from the pastures of the Danube to assimilate the culture of the highly civilized regions in which they first appeared as barbarian destroyers. They accepted the industrial arts of the eastern Mediterranean, adopted the Phœnician alphabet, and emulated the Phœnician merchant. By the seventh century before our era they had towns, colonies, and commerce, with much stimulating running hither and thither. We get our first traces of new intellectual enterprise in the Ionian cities, especially Miletus, and in the Italian colonies of the Greeks. Only

BEGINNING OF CRITICAL THINKING

later did Athens become the unrivaled center in a marvelous outflowering of the human intelligence.

It is a delicate task to summarize what we owe to the Greeks. Leaving aside their supreme achievements in literature and art, we can consider only very briefly the general scope and nature of their thinking as it relates most closely to our theme.

The chief strength of the Greeks lay in their freedom from hampering intellectual tradition. They had no venerated classics, no holy books, no dead languages to master, no authorities to check their free speculation. As Lord Bacon reminds us, they had no antiquity of knowledge and no knowledge of antiquity. A modern classicist would have been a forlorn outlander in ancient Athens, with no books in a forgotten tongue, no obsolete inflections to impose upon reluctant youth. He would have had to use the everyday speech of the sandal-maker and fuller.

For a long time no technical words were invented to give aloofness and seeming precision to philosophic and scientific discussion. Aristotle was the first to use words incomprehensible to the average citizen. It was in these conditions that the possibilities of human criticism first showed themselves. The primitive notions of man, of the gods, and of the workings of natural forces began to be overhauled on an entirely new scale. Intelligence developed rapidly as exceptionally bold individuals came to have their suspicions of simple, spontaneous, and ancient ways of looking at things. Ultimately there came men who professed to doubt everything.

As Abelard long after put it, "By doubting we come to question, and by seeking we may come upon the truth." But man is by nature credulous. He is victimized by first impressions, from which he can only escape with great difficulty. He resents criticism of accepted and familiar ideas as he resents any unwelcome disturbance of routine. So criticism is against nature, for it conflicts with the smooth workings of our more primitive minds, those of the child and the savage.

It should not be forgotten that the Greek people were no exception in this matter. Anaxagoras and Aristotle were banished for thinking as they did; Euripides was an object of abhorrence to the conservative of his day, and Socrates was actually executed for his godless teachings. The Greek thinkers furnish the first instance of intellectual freedom, of the "self-detachment and self-abnegating vigor of criticism" which is most touchingly illustrated in the honest "know-nothingism" of Socrates. *They discovered skepticism in the higher and proper significance of the word, and this was their supreme contribution to human thought.*

One of the finest examples of early Greek skepticism was the discovery of Xenophanes that man created the gods in his own image. He looked about him, observed the current conceptions of the gods, compared those of different peoples, and reached the conclusion that the way in which a tribe pictured its gods was not the outcome of any knowledge of how they really looked and whether they had black eyes or blue, but was a reflection of the familiarly human. If the lions had gods they would have the shape of their worshipers.

No more fundamentally shocking revelation was ever made than this, for it shook the very foundations of religious belief. The home life on Olympus as described in Homer was too scandalous to escape the attention of the thoughtful, and no later Christian could have denounced the demoralizing influence of the current religious beliefs in hotter indignation than did Plato. To judge from the reflection of Greek thought which we find in Lucretius and Cicero, none of the primitive religious beliefs escaped mordant criticism.

The second great discovery of the Greek thinkers was *metaphysics*. They did not have the name, which originated long after in quite an absurd fashion,[1] but they reveled in the thing. Nowadays metaphysics is revered by some as our noblest effort to reach the highest truth, and scorned by others as the silliest of wild-goose chases. I am inclined to rate it, like smoking, as a highly gratifying indulgence to those who like it, and, as indulgences go, relatively innocent. The Greeks found that the mind could carry on an absorbing game with itself. We all engage in reveries and fantasies of a homely, everyday type, concerned with our desires or resentments, but the fantasy of the metaphysician busies itself with conceptions, abstractions, distinctions, hypotheses, postulates, and logical inferences. Having made certain postulates or hypotheses, he finds new conclusions, which he follows in a seemingly convincing manner. This gives him the delightful emotion of pursuing Truth, something as the simple man pursues a

---

[1] When in the time of Cicero the long-hidden works of Aristotle were recovered and put into the hands of Andronicus of Rhodes to edit, he found certain fragments of highly abstruse speculation which he did not know what to do with. So he called them "addenda to the Physics"—*Ta meta ta physica*. These fragments, under the caption "Metaphysica," became the most revered of Aristotle's productions, his "First Philosophy," as the Scholastics were wont to call it.

maiden. Only Truth is more elusive than the maiden and may continue to beckon her follower for long years, no matter how gray and doddering he may become.

Let me give two examples of metaphysical reasoning.[1] We have an idea of an omnipotent, all-good, and perfect being. We are incapable, knowing as we do only imperfect things, of framing such an idea for ourselves, so it must have been given us by the being himself. And perfection must include existence, so God must exist. This was good enough for Anselm and for Descartes, who went on to build a whole closely concatenated philosophical system on this foundation. To them the logic seemed irrefragable; to the modern student of comparative religion, even to Kant, himself a metaphysician, there was nothing whatsoever in it but an illustration of the native operations of a mind that has made a wholly gratuitous hypothesis and is victimized by an orderly series of spontaneous associations.

A second example of metaphysics may be

---

[1] John Dewey deduces metaphysics from man's original reverie and then shows how in time it became a solemn form of rationalizing current habits and standards. *Reconstruction in Philosophy*, lectures i–ii. It is certainly surprising how few philosophical writers have ever reached other than perfectly commonplace conclusions in regard to practical "morality."

found in the doctrines of the Eleatic philosophers, who early appeared in the Greek colonies on the coast of Italy, and thought hard about space and motion. Empty space seemed as good as nothing, and, as nothing could not be said to exist, space must be an illusion; and as motion implied space in which to take place, there could be no motion. So all things were really perfectly compact and at rest, and all our impressions of change were the illusions of the thoughtless and the simple-minded. Since one of the chief satisfactions of the metaphysicians is to get away from the welter of our mutable world into a realm of assurance, this doctrine exercised a great fascination over many minds. The Eleatic conviction of unchanging stability received a new form in Plato's doctrine of eternal "ideas," and later developed into the comforting conception of the "Absolute," in which logical and world-weary souls have sought refuge from the times of Plotinus to those of Josiah Royce.

But there was one group of Greek thinkers whose general notions of natural operations correspond in a striking manner to the conclusions of the most recent science. These were the Epicureans. Democritus was in no way a modern experimental scientist, but he met the Eleatic metaphysics with another set of speculative considerations which happened to be nearer what is now regarded as the truth than theirs. He rejected the Eleatic decisions against the reality of space and motion on the ground that, since motion obviously took place, the void must be a reality, even if the metaphysician could not conceive it. He hit upon the notion that all things were composed of minute, indestructible particles (or atoms) of fixed kinds. Given motion and sufficient time, these might by fortuitous concourse make all possible combinations. And it was one of these combinations which we call the world as we find it. For the atoms of various shapes were inherently capable of making up all material things, even the soul of man and the gods themselves. There was no permanence anywhere; all was no more than the shifting accidental and fleeting combinations of the permanent atoms of which the cosmos was composed. This doctrine was accepted by the noble Epicurus and his school and is delivered to us in the immortal poem of Lucretius "On the Nature of Things."

The Epicureans believed the gods to exist because, like Anselm and Descartes, they thought we had an innate idea of them.

But the divine beings led a life of elegant ease and took no account of man; neither his supplications, nor his sweet-smelling sacrifices, nor his blasphemies, ever disturbed their calm. Moreover, the human soul was dissipated at death. So the Epicureans flattered themselves that they had delivered man from his two chief apprehensions, the fear of the gods and the fear of death. For, as Lucretius says, he who understands the real nature of things will see that both are the illusions of ignorance. Thus one school of Greek thinkers attained to a complete rejection of religious beliefs in the name of natural science.

9. Influence of Plato and Aristotle

In Plato we have at once the skepticism and the metaphysics of his contemporaries. He has had his followers down through the ages, some of whom carried his skepticism to its utmost bounds, while others availed themselves of his metaphysics to rear a system of arrogant mystical dogmatism. He put his speculations in the form of dialogues —ostensible discussions in the market place or the houses of philosophic Athenians. The Greek word for logic is *dialectic*, which really means "discussion," argumentation in the interest of fuller analysis, with the hope of more critical conclusions. The dialogues are the drama of his day, employed in Plato's magical hand as a vehicle of discursive reason. Of late we have in Ibsen, Shaw, Brieux, and Galsworthy the old expedient applied to the consideration of social perplexities and contradictions. The dialogue is indecisive in its outcome. It does not lend itself to dogmatic conclusions and systematic presentation, but exposes the intricacy of all important questions and the inevitable conflict of views, which may seem altogether irreconcilable. We much need to encourage and elaborate opportunities for profitable discussion to-day. We should revert to the dialectic of the Athenian agora and make it a chosen instrument for clarifying, co-ordinating and directing our co-operative thinking.

Plato's indecision and urbane fair-mindedness is called irony. Now irony is seriousness without solemnity. It assumes that man is a serio-comic animal, and that no treatment of his affairs can be appropriate which gives him a consistency and dignity which he does not possess. He is always a child and a savage. He is the victim of conflicting desires and hidden yearnings. He may talk like a sentimental idealist and act like a brute. The same person will devote anxious years to the invention of high explosives and then give his fortune to the promotion of peace. We devise the most exquisite machinery for blowing our neighbors to pieces and then display our highest skill and organization in trying to patch together such as offer hope of being mended. Our nature forbids us to make a definite choice between the machine gun and the Red Cross nurse. So we use the one to keep the other busy. Human thought and conduct can only be treated broadly and truly in a mood of tolerant irony. It belies the logical precision of the long-faced, humorless writer on politics and ethics, whose works rarely deal with man at all, but are a stupid form of metaphysics.

Plato made terms with the welter of things, but sought relief in the conception of supernal models, eternal in the heavens, after which all things were imperfectly fashioned. He confessed that he could not bear to accept a world which was like a leaky pot or a man running at the nose. In short, he ascribed the highest form of existence to ideals and abstractions. This was a new and sophisticated republication of savage animism. It invited lesser minds than his to indulge in all sorts of noble vagueness and impertinent jargon

PLATO AND ARISTOTLE

which continue to curse our popular discussions of human affairs. He consecrated one of the chief foibles of the human mind and elevated it to a religion.

Ever since his time men have discussed the import of names. Are there such things as love, friendship, and honor, or are there only lovely things, friendly emotions in this individual and that, deeds which we may, according to our standards, pronounce honorable or dishonorable? If you believe in beauty, truth, and love *as such* you are a Platonist. If you believe that there are only individual instances and illustrations of various classified emotions and desires and acts, and that abstractions are only the inevitable categories of thought, you would in the Middle Ages have been called a "nominalist."

This matter merits a long discussion, but one can test any book or newspaper editorial at his leisure and see whether the writer puts you off with abstractions—Americanism, Bolshevism, public welfare, liberty, national honor, religion, morality, good taste, rights of man, science, reason, error—or, on the other hand, casts some light on actual human complications. I do not mean, of course, that we can get along without the use of abstract and general terms in our thinking and speaking, but we should be on our constant guard against viewing them as forces and attributing to them the vigor of personality. <u>Animism</u> is, as already explained, a pitfall which is always yawning before us and into which we are sure to plunge unless we are ever watchful. <u>Platonism is its most amiable and complete disguise.</u>

Previous to Aristotle, Greek thought had been wonderfully free and elastic. It had not settled into compartments or assumed an educational form which would secure its unrevised transmission from teacher to student. It was not gathered together in systematic treatises. Aristotle combined the supreme powers of an original and creative thinker with the impulses of a textbook writer. He loved order and classification. He supplied manuals of Ethics, Politics, Logic, Psychology, Physics, Metaphysics, Economics, Poetics, Zoölogy, Meteorology, Constitutional Law, and God only knows what not, for we do not have by any means all the things he wrote. And he was equally interested, and perhaps equally capable, in all the widely scattered fields in which he labored. And some of his manuals were so overwhelming in the conclusiveness of their reasoning, so all-embracing in their scope, that the mediæval universities may be forgiven for having made them the sole basis of a liberal education and for imposing fines on those who ventured to differ from "The Philosopher." He seemed to know everything that could be known and to have ordered all earthly knowledge in an inspired codification which would stand the professors in good stead down to the day of judgment.

Aristotle combined an essentially metaphysical taste with a preternatural power of observation in dealing with the workings of nature. In spite of his inevitable mistakes, which became the curse of later docile generations, no other thinker of whom we have record can really compare with him in the distinction and variety of his achievements. It is not his fault that posterity used his works to hamper further progress and clarification. He is the father of book knowledge and the grandfather of the commentator.

After two or three hundred years of talking in the market place and of philosophic discussions prolonged until morning, such of the Greeks as were predisposed to speculation had thought all the thoughts and uttered all the criticisms of commonly accepted beliefs and of one another that could by any possibility occur to those who had little inclination to fare forth and extend their knowledge of the so-called realities of nature by painful and specialized research and examination. This is to me the chief reason why, except for some advances in mathematics, astronomy, geography, and the refinements of scholarship, the glorious period of the Greek mind is commonly and rightfully assumed to have come to an end about the time of Aristotle's death. Why did the Greeks not go on, as modern scientists have gone on, with vistas of the unachieved still ahead of them?

In the first place, Greek civilization was founded on slavery and a fixed condition of the industrial arts. The philosopher and scholar was estopped from fumbling with those everyday processes that were associated with the mean life of the slave and servant. Consequently there was no one to devise the practical apparatus by which alone profound and ever-increasing knowledge of natural operations is possible. The mechanical inventiveness of the Greeks was slight, and hence they never came upon the lens; they had no microscope to reveal the minute, no telescope to attract the remote; they never devised a mechanical timepiece, a thermometer, nor a barometer, to say nothing of cameras and spectroscopes. Archimedes, it is reported, disdained to make any record of his ingenious devices, for they were unworthy the noble profession of a philosopher. Such inventions as were made were usually either toys or of a heavy practical character. So the next great step forward in the extension of the human mind awaited the disappearance of slavery and the slowly dawning suspicion, and final repudiation, of the older metaphysics, which first became marked some three hundred years ago.

V

V

And God made the two great lights; the greater light to rule the day, and the lesser light to rule the night; he made the stars also. And God set them in the firmament of heaven to give light upon the earth.

And God said, Let the earth bring forth the living creature after its kind, cattle and creeping thing, and beast of the earth after its kind: and it was so.

And God said, Let us make man in our image, after our likeness: and let them have dominion over the fish of the sea, and over the fowl of the air, and over the cattle, and over all the earth, and over every creeping thing that creepeth upon the earth.—Gen. i.

Ibi vacabimus et videbimus, videbimus et amabimus, amabimus et laudabimus. Ecce quod erit in fine sine fine. Nam quis alius noster est finis nisi pervenire ad regnum, cuius nullus est finis?—AUGUSTINE.

10. Origin of Mediæval Civilization

IN the formation of what we may call our historical mind—namely, that modification of our animal and primitive outlook which has been produced by men of exceptional intellectual venturesomeness—the Greeks played a great part. We have seen how the Greek thinkers introduced for the first time highly subtle and critical ways of scrutinizing old beliefs, and how they disabused their minds of many an ancient and naïve mistake. But our current ways of thinking are not derived directly from the Greeks; we are separated from them by the Roman Empire and the Middle Ages. When we think of Athens we think of the Parthenon and its frieze, of Sophocles and Euripides, of Socrates and Plato and Aristotle, of urbanity and clarity and moderation in all things. When we think of the Middle Ages we find ourselves in a world of monks, martyrs, and miracles, of popes and emperors, of knights and ladies; we remember Gregory the Great, Abélard, and Thomas Aquinas—and very little do these reminiscences have in common with those of Hellas.

It was indeed a different world, with quite different fundamental presuppositions. Marvelous as were the achievements of the Greeks in art and literature, and ingenious as they were in new and varied combinations of ideas, they paid too little attention to the common things of the world to devise the necessary means of penetrating its mysteries. They failed to come upon the lynx-eyed lens, or other instruments of modern investigation, and thus never gained a godlike vision of the remote and the minute. Their critical thought was consequently not grounded in experimental or applied science, and without that the western world was unable to advance or even long maintain their high standards of criticism.

After the Hellenes were absorbed into the vast Roman Empire critical thought and creative intelligence—rare and precarious things at best—began to decline, at first slowly and then with fatal rapidity and completeness. Moreover, new and highly uncritical beliefs and modes of thought became popular. They came from the Near East—Mesopotamia, Syria, Egypt, and Asia Minor—and largely supplanted the critical traditions of the great schools of Greek philosophy. The Stoic and Epicurean dogmas had lost their freshness. The Greek thinkers had all agreed in looking for salvation through intelligence and knowledge. But eloquent leaders arose to reveal a new salvation, and over the portal of truth they erased the word "Reason" and wrote "Faith" in its stead; and the people listened gladly to the new prophets, for it was necessary only *to believe* to be saved, and believing is far easier than thinking.

It was religious and mystical thought which, in contrast to the secular philosophy of the Greeks and the scientific thought of our own day, dominated the intellectual life of the Middle Ages.

Before considering this new phase through which the human mind was to pass it is necessary to guard against a common misapprehension in the use of the term "Middle Ages." Our historical textbooks usually include in that period the happenings between the dissolution of the Roman Empire and the voyages of Columbus or the opening of the Protestant revolt. To the student of intellectual history this is unfortunate, for the simple reason that almost all the ideas and even institutions of the Middle Ages, such as the church and monasticism and organized religious intolerance, really originated in the late Roman Empire. Moreover, the intellectual revolution which has ushered in the thought of our day did not get well under way until the seventeenth century. So one may say that mediæval thought began long before the accepted beginning of the Middle Ages and persisted a century or so after they are ordinarily esteemed to have come to an end. We have to continue to employ the old expression for convenience' sake, but from the standpoint of the history of the European mind three periods should be distinguished, lying between ancient Greek thought as it was flourishing in Athens, Alexandria, Rhodes, Rome, and elsewhere at the opening of the Christian era, and the birth of modern science some sixteen hundred years later.

The first of these is the period of the Christian Fathers, culminating in the authoritative writings of Augustine, who died in 430. By this time a great part of the critical Greek books had disappeared in western Europe. As for pagan writers, one has difficulty in thinking of a single name (except that of Lucian) later than Juvenal, who had died nearly three hundred years before Augustine. Worldly knowledge was reduced to pitiful compendiums on which the mediæval students were later to place great reliance. Scientific, literary, and historical information was scarcely to be had. The western world, so far as it thought at all, devoted its attention to religion and all manner of mystical ideas, old and new. As Harnack has so well said, the world was already intellectually bankrupt before the German invasions and their accompanying disorders plunged it into still deeper ignorance and mental obscurity.

The second, or "Dark Age," lasted with only slight improvement from Augustine to Abélard, about seven hundred years. The prosperous *villas* disappeared; towns vanished or shriveled up; libraries were burned or rotted away from neglect; schools were closed, to be reopened later here and there, after Charlemagne's educational edict, in an especially enterprising monastery or by some exceptional bishop who did not spend his whole time in fighting.

From about the year 1100 conditions began to be more and more favorable to the revival of intellectual ambition, a recovery of forgotten knowledge, and a gradual accumulation of new information and inventions unknown to the Greeks, or indeed to any previous civilization. The main presuppositions of this third period of the later Middle Ages go back, however, to the Roman Empire. They had been formulated by the Church Fathers, transmitted through the Dark Age, and were now elaborated by the professors in the newly established universities under the influence of Aristotle's recovered works and built up into a majestic intellectual structure known as Scholasticism. On these mediæval university professors—the schoolmen—Lord Bacon long ago pronounced a judgment that may well stand to-day. "Having sharp and strong wits, and abundance of leisure, and small variety of reading, but their wits being shut up in the cells of a few authors (chiefly Aristotle, their dictator), as their persons were shut up in the cells of monasteries and colleges, and knowing little history, either of nature or time [they], did out of no great quantity of matter and infinite agitation of wit spin out unto us those laborious webs of learning which are extant in their books."

Our civilization and the human mind, critical and uncritical, as we now find it in our western world, is a direct and uninterrupted outgrowth of the civilization and thought of the later Middle Ages. Very gradually only did peculiarly free and audacious individual thinkers escape from this or that mediæval belief, until in our own day some few have come to reject practically all the presuppositions on which the Scholastic system was reared. But the great mass of Christian believers, whether

Catholic or Protestant, still professedly or implicitly adhere to the assumptions of the Middle Ages, at least in all matters in which religious or moral sanctions are concerned. It is true that outside the Catholic clergy the term "mediæval" is often used in a sense of disparagement, but that should not blind us to the fact that mediæval presumptions, whether for better or worse, are still common. A few of the most fundamental of these presuppositions especially germane to our theme may be pointed out here.

11. Our Mediæval Intellectual Inheritance

The Greeks and Romans had various theories of the origin of things, all vague and admittedly conjectural. But the Christians, relying upon the inspired account in the Bible, built their theories on information which they believed vouchsafed to them by God himself. Their whole conception of human history was based upon a far more fundamental and thorough supernaturalism than we find among the Greeks and Romans. The pagan philosophers reckoned with the gods, to be sure, but they never assumed that man's earthly life should turn entirely on what was to happen after death. This was in theory the sole preoccupation of the mediæval Christian. Life here below was but a brief, if decisive, preliminary to the real life to come.

The mediæval Christian was essentially more polytheistic than his pagan predecessors, for he pictured hierarchies of good and evil spirits who were ever aiding him to reach heaven or seducing him into the paths of sin and error. Miracles were of common occurrence and might be attributed either to God or the devil; the direct intervention of both good and evil spirits played a conspicuous part in the explanation of daily acts and motives.[1]

As a distinguished church historian has said, the God of the Middle Ages was a God of arbitrariness—the more arbitrary the more Godlike. By frequent interferences with the regular course of events he made his existence clear, reassured his children of his continued solicitude, and frustrated the plots of the Evil One. Not until the eighteenth century did any considerable number of thinkers revolt against this conception of the Deity and come

---

[1] St. Ethelred, returning from a pious visit to Citeaux in the days of Henry II, encountered a great storm when he reached the Channel. He asked himself what *he* had done to be thus delayed, and suddenly thought that he had failed to fulfill a promise to write a poem on St. Cuthbert. When he had completed this, "wonderful to say, the sea ceased to rage and became tranquil."—*Surtees Society Publications*, i, p. 177.

to worship a God of orderliness who abode by his own laws.

The mediæval thinkers all accepted without question what Santayana has strikingly described as the "Christian Epic." This included the general historical conceptions of how man came about, and how, in view of his origin and his past, he should conduct his life. The universe had come into being in less than a week, and man had originally been created in a state of perfection along with all other things—sun, moon, and stars, plants and animals. After a time the first human pair had yielded to temptation, transgressed God's commands, and been driven from the lovely garden in which he had placed them. So sin came into the world, and the offspring of the guilty pair were thereby contaminated and defiled from the womb.

In time the wickedness became such on the newly created earth that God resolved to blot out mankind, excepting only Noah's family, which was spared to repeople the earth after the Flood, but the unity of language that man had formerly possessed was lost. At the appointed time, preceded by many prophetic visions among the chosen people, God sent his Son to live the life of men on earth and become their Saviour by submitting to death. Thereafter, with the spread of the gospel, the struggle between the kingdom of God and that of the devil became the supreme conflict of history. It was to culminate in the Last Judgment, when the final separation of good and evil should take place and the blessed should ascend into the heavens to dwell with God forever, while the wicked sank to hell to writhe in endless torment.

This general account of man, his origin and fate, embraced in the Christian Epic, was notable for its precision, its divine authenticity, and the obstacles which its authority consequently presented to any revision in the light of increasing knowledge. The fundamental truths in regard to man were assumed to be established once and for all. The Greek thinkers had had little in the way of authority on which to build, and no inconsiderable number of them frankly confessed that they did not believe that such a thing could exist for the thoroughly sophisticated intelligence. But mediæval philosophy and science *were grounded wholly in authority*. The mediæval schoolmen turned aside from the hard path of skepticism, long searchings and investigation of actual phenomena, and confidently believed that they could find

OUR MEDIÆVAL INHERITANCE

truth by the easy way of revelation and the elaboration of unquestioned dogmas.

This reliance on authority is a fundamental primitive trait. We have inherited it not only from our mediæval forefathers, but, like them and through them, from long generations of prehistoric men. We all have a natural tendency to rely upon established beliefs and fixed institutions. This is an expression of our spontaneous confidence in everything that comes to us in an unquestioned form. As children we are subject to authority and cannot escape the control of existing opinion. We unconsciously absorb our ideas and views from the group in which we happen to live. What we see about us, what we are told, and what we read has to be received at its face value so long as there are no conflicts to arouse skepticism.

We are tremendously suggestible. Our mechanism is much better adapted to credulity than to questioning. All of us *believe* nearly all the time. Few doubt, and only now and then. The past exercises an almost irresistible fascination over us. As children we learn to look up to the old, and when we grow up we do not permit our poignant realization of elderly incapacity among our contemporaries to rouse suspicions of Moses,

Isaiah, Confucius, or Aristotle. Their sayings come to us unquestioned; their remoteness makes inquiry into their competence impossible. We readily assume that they had sources of information and wisdom superior to the prophets of our own day.

During the Middle Ages reverence for authority, and for that particular form of authority which we may call the tyranny of the past, was dominant, but probably not more so than it had been in other societies and ages—in ancient Egypt, in China and India. Of the great sources of mediæval authority, the Bible and the Church Fathers, the Roman and Church law, and the encyclopædic writings of Aristotle, none continues nowadays to hold us in its old grip. Even the Bible, although nominally unquestioned among Roman Catholics and all the more orthodox Protestant sects, is rarely appealed to, as of old, in parliamentary debate or in discussions of social and economic questions. It is still a religious authority, but it no longer forms the basis of secular decisions.

The findings of modern science have shaken the hold of the sources of mediæval authority, but they have done little as yet to loosen our inveterate habit of relying on the more insidious authority of current practice and belief. We still assume that received dogmas represent the secure conclusions of mankind, and that current institutions represent the approved results of much experiment in the past, which it would be worse than futile to repeat. One solemn remembrancer will cite as a warning the discreditable experience of the Greek cities in democracy; another, how the decline of "morality" and the disintegration of the family heralded the fall of Rome; another, the constant menace of mob rule as exemplified in the Reign of Terror.

But to the student of history these alleged illustrations have little bearing on present conditions. He is struck, moreover, with the ease with which ancient misapprehensions are transmitted from generation to generation and with the difficulty of launching a newer and clearer and truer idea of anything. Bacon warns us that the multitude, "or the wisest for the multitude's sake," is in reality "ready to give passage rather to that which is popular and superficial than to that which is substantial and profound; for the truth is that time seemeth to be of the nature of a river or stream, which carrieth down to us that which is light and blown up, and sinketh and drowneth that which is weighty and solid."

It is very painful to most minds to admit that the past does not furnish us with reliable, permanent standards of conduct and of public policy. We resent the imputation that things are not going, on the whole, pretty well, and find excuses for turning our backs on disconcerting and puzzling facts. We are full of respectable fears and a general timidity in the face of conditions which we vaguely feel are escaping control in spite of our best efforts to prevent any thoroughgoing readjustment. We instinctively try to show that Mr. Keynes must surely be wrong about the Treaty of Versailles; that Mr. Gibbs must be perversely exaggerating the horrors of modern war; that Mr. Hobson certainly views the industrial crisis with unjustifiable pessimism; that "business as usual" cannot be that socially perverse and incredibly inexpedient thing Mr. Veblen shows it to be; that Mr. Robin's picture of Lenin can only be explained by a disguised sympathy for Bolshevism.

Yet, even if we could assume that traditional opinion is a fairly clear and reliable reflection of hard-earned experience, surely it should have less weight in our day and generation than in the past. For changes have overtaken mankind which have fundamentally altered the conditions in which we live, and which are revolutionizing the relations between individuals and classes and nations. Moreover, we must remember that knowledge has widened and deepened, so that, could any of us really catch up with the information of our own time, he would have little temptation to indulge the mediæval habit of appealing to the authority of the past.

The Christian Epic did not have to rely for its perpetuation either on its intellectual plausibility or its traditional authority. During the Middle Ages there developed a vast and powerful religious State, the mediæval Church, the real successor, as Hobbes pointed out, to the Roman Empire; and the Church with all its resources, including its control over "the secular arm" of kings and princes, was ready to defend the Christian beliefs against question and revision. To doubt the teachings of the Church was the supreme crime; it was treason against God himself, in comparison with which—to judge from mediæval experts on heresy—murder was a minor offense.

We do not, however, inherit our present disposition to intolerance solely from the Middle Ages. As animals and children and savages, we are naïvely and unquestioningly intolerant. All divergence from the customary is suspicious and repugnant. It seems perverse, and readily suggests evil intentions. Indeed, so natural and spontaneous is intolerance that the question of freedom of speech and writing scarcely became a real issue before the seventeenth century. We have seen that some of the Greek thinkers were banished, or even executed, for their new ideas. The Roman officials, as well as the populace, pestered the early Christians, not so much for the substance of their views as because they were puritanical, refused the routine reverence to the gods, and prophesied the downfall of the State.

But with the firm establishment of Christianity edicts began to be issued by the Roman emperors making orthodox Christian belief the test of good citizenship. One who disagreed with the emperor and his religious advisers in regard to the relation of the three members of the Trinity was subject to prosecution. Heretical books were burned, the houses of heretics destroyed. So, organized mediæval religious intolerance was, like so many other things, a heritage of the later Roman Empire, and was duly sanctioned in both the Theodosian and Justinian Codes. It was, however, with the Inquisition, beginning in the thirteenth century, that the intol-

OUR MEDIÆVAL INHERITANCE

erance of the Middle Ages reached its most perfect organization.

Heresy was looked upon as a contagious disease that must be checked at all costs. It did not matter that the heretic usually led a conspicuously blameless life, that he was arduous, did not swear, was emaciated with fasting and refused to participate in the vain recreations of his fellows. He was, indeed, overserious and took his religion too hard. This offensive parading as an angel of light was explained as the devil's camouflage. No one tried to find out what the heretic really thought or what were the merits of his divergent beliefs. Because he insisted on expressing his conception of God in slightly unfamiliar terms, the heretic was often branded as an atheist, just as to-day the Socialist is so often accused of being opposed to all government, when the real objection to him is that he believes in too much government. It was sufficient to classify a suspected heretic as an Albigensian, or Waldensian, or a member of some other heretical sect. There was no use in his trying to explain or justify; it was enough that he diverged.

There have been various explanations of mediæval religious intolerance. Lecky, for example, thought that it was due to the <u>theory of exclusive salvation</u>; that, since there was only one way of getting to heaven, all should obviously be compelled to adopt it, for the saving of their souls from eternal torment. But one finds little solicitude for the damned in mediæval writings. The public at large thought hell none too bad for one who revolted against God and Holy Church. No, the heretics were persecuted because heresy was, according to the notions of the time, a monstrous and unutterably wicked thing, and because their beliefs threatened the vested interests of that day.

We now realize more clearly than did Lecky that the <u>Church was really a State in the Middle Ages</u>, with its own laws and courts and prisons and regular taxation to which all were subject. It had all the interests and all the touchiness of a State, and more. The heretic was a traitor and a rebel. He thought that he could get along without the pope and bishops, and that he could well spare the ministrations of the orthodox priests and escape their exactions. He was the "anarchist," the "Red" of his time, who was undermining established authority, and, with the approval of all right-minded citizens, he was treated accordingly. For the mediæval citizen no more conceived of a State in which the Church was not the dominating authority than we can conceive of a society in which the present political State may have been superseded by some other form of organization.

Yet the inconceivable has come to pass. Secular authority has superseded in nearly all matters the old ecclesiastical regime. What was the supreme issue of the Middle Ages—the distinction between the religious heretic and the orthodox—is the least of public questions now.

What, then, we may ask, has been the outcome of the old religious persecutions, of the trials, tortures, imprisonings, burnings, and massacres, culminating with the Revocation of the Edict of Nantes? What did the Inquisition and the censorship, both so long unquestioned, accomplish? Did they succeed in defending the truth or "safeguarding" society? At any rate, conformity was not established. Nor did the Holy Roman Church maintain its monopoly, although it has survived, purified and freed from many an ancient abuse. In most countries of western Europe and in our own land one may now believe as he wishes, teach such religious views as appeal to him, and join with others who share his sympathies. "Atheism" is still a shocking charge in many ears, but the atheist is no longer an outlaw. *It has been demonstrated, in short, that religious dogma can be neglected in matters of public concern and reduced to a question of private taste and preference.*

This is an incredible revolution. But we have many reasons for suspecting that in a much shorter time than that which has elapsed since the Inquisition was founded, the present attempt to eliminate by force those who contemplate a fundamental reordering of social and economic relations will seem quite as inexpedient and hopeless as the Inquisition's effort to defend the monopoly of the mediæval Church.

We can learn much from the past in regard to wrong ways of dealing with new ideas. As yet we have only old-fashioned and highly expensive modes of meeting the inevitable changes which are bound to take place. Repression has now and then enjoyed some temporary success, it is true, but in the main it has failed lamentably and produced only suffering and confusion. Much will depend on whether our purpose is to keep things as they are or to bring about readjustments designed to correct abuses and injustice in the present order. Do we believe, in other words, that truth is finally established and

OUR MEDIÆVAL INHERITANCE

that we have only to defend it, or that it is still in the making? Do we believe in what is commonly called progress, or do we think of that as belonging only to the past? Have we, on the whole, arrived, or are we only on the way, or mayhap just starting?

In the Middle Ages, even in the times of the Greeks and Romans, there was little or no conception of progress as the word is now used. There could doubtless be improvement in detail. Men could be wiser and better or more ignorant and perverse. But the assumption was that in general the social, economic, and religious order was fairly standardized.

This was especially true in the Middle Ages. During these centuries men's single objective was the assurance of heaven and escape from hell. Life was an angry river into which men were cast. Demons were on every hand to drag them down. The only aim could be, with God's help, to reach the celestial shore. There was no time to consider whether the river might be made less dangerous by concerted effort, through the deflection of its torrents and the removal of its sharpest rocks. No one thought that human efforts should be directed to making the lot of humanity progressively better by intelligent reforms in the light of advancing knowledge.

The world was a place to escape from on the best terms possible. In our own day this mediæval idea of a static society yields only grudgingly, and the notion of inevitable vital change is as yet far from assimilated. We confess it with our lips, but resist it in our hearts. We have learned as yet to respect only one class of fundamental innovators, those dedicated to natural science and its applications. The social innovator is still generally suspect.

To the mediæval theologian, man was by nature vile. We have seen that, according to the Christian Epic, he was assoiled from birth with the primeval sin of his first parents, and began to darken his score with fresh offenses of his own as soon as he became intelligent enough to do so. An elaborate mechanism was supplied by the Church for washing away the original pollution and securing forgiveness for later sins. Indeed, this was ostensibly its main business.

We may still well ask, Is man by nature bad? And accordingly as we answer the question we either frame appropriate means for frustrating his evil tendencies or, if we see some promise in him, work for his freedom and bid him take advantage of it to make himself and others happy. So far as I know, Charron, a friend of Montaigne, was one of the first to say a good word for man's animal nature, and a hundred years later the amiable Shaftesbury pointed out some honestly gentlemanly traits in the species. To the modern student of biology and anthropology man is neither good nor bad. There is no longer any "mystery of evil." But the mediæval notion of *sin*—a term heavy with mysticism and deserving of careful scrutiny by every thoughtful person—still confuses us.

Of man's impulses, the one which played the greatest part in mediæval thoughts of sin and in the monastic ordering of life was the sexual. The presuppositions of the Middle Ages in the matter of the relations of men and women have been carried over to our own day. As compared with many of the ideas which we have inherited from the past, they are of comparatively recent origin. The Greeks and Romans were, on the whole, primitive and uncritical in their view of sex. The philosophers do not seem to have speculated on sex, although there was evidently some talk in Athens of women's rights. The movement is satirized by Aristophanes, and later Plato showed a willingness in *The Republic* to impeach the current notions of the family and women's position in general.

But there are few traces of our ideas of

sexual "purity" in the classical writers. To the Stoic philosopher, and to other thoughtful elderly people, sexual indulgence was deemed a low order of pleasure and one best carefully controlled in the interests of peace of mind. But with the incoming of Christianity an essentially new attitude developed, which is still, consciously or unconsciously, that of most people to-day.

St. Augustine, who had led a free life as a teacher of rhetoric in Carthage and Rome, came in his later years to believe, as he struggled to overcome his youthful temptations, that sexual desire was the most devilish of man's enemies and the chief sign of his degradation. He could imagine no such unruly urgence in man's perfect estate, when Adam and Eve still dwelt in Paradise. But with man's fall sexual desire appeared as the sign and seal of human debasement. This theory is poignantly set forth in Augustine's *City of God*. He furnished therein a philosophy for the monks, and doubtless his fourteenth book was well thumbed by those who were wont to ponder somewhat wistfully on one of the sins they had fled the world to escape.

Christian monasticism was spreading in western Europe in Augustine's time, and the monkist vows included "chastity." There followed a long struggle to force the whole priesthood to adopt a celibate life, and this finally succeeded so far as repeated decrees of the Church could effect it. Marriage was proper for the laity, but both the monastic and secular clergy aspired to a superior holiness which should banish all thoughts of fervent earthly love. Thus a highly unnatural life was accepted by men and women of the most varied temperament and often with slight success.

The result of Augustine's theories and of the efforts to frustrate one of man's most vehement impulses was to give sex a conscious importance it had never possessed before. The devil was thrust out of the door only to come in at all the windows. In due time the Protestant sects abolished monasteries, and the Catholic countries later followed their example. The Protestant clergy were permitted to marry, and the old asceticism has visibly declined. But it has done much to determine our whole attitude toward sex, and there is no class of questions still so difficult to discuss with full honesty or to deal with critically and with an open mind as those relating to the intimate relations of men and women.

No one familiar with mediæval literature will, however, be inclined to accuse its authors of prudishness. Nevertheless, modern prudishness, as it prevails especially in England and the United States—our squeamish and shamefaced reluctance to recognize and deal frankly with the facts and problems of sex—is clearly an outgrowth of the mediæval attitude which looked on sexual impulse as of evil origin and a sign of man's degradation. Modern psychologists have shown that prudishness is not always an indication of exceptional purity, but rather the reverse. It is often a disguise thrown over repressed sexual interest and sexual preoccupations. It appears to be decreasing among the better educated of the younger generation. The study of biology, and especially of embryology, is an easy and simple way of disintegrating the "impurity complex." "Purity" in the sense of ignorance and suppressed curiosity is a highly dangerous state of mind. And such purity in alliance with prudery and defensive hypocrisy makes any honest discussion or essential readjustment of our institutions and habits extremely difficult.

One of the greatest contrasts between mediæval thinking and the more critical thought of to-day lies in the general conception of man's relation to the cosmos. To the mediæval philosopher, as to the stupidest serf of the time, the world was made for man. All the heavenly bodies revolved about man's abode as their center. All creatures were made to assist or to try man. God and the devil were preoccupied with his fate, for had not God made him in his own image for his glory, and was not the devil intent on populating his own infernal kingdom? It was easy for those who had a poetic turn of mind to think of nature's workings as symbols for man's edification. The habits of the lion or the eagle yielded moral lessons or illustrated the divine scheme of salvation. Even the written word was to be valued, not for what it seemed to say, but for hidden allegories depicting man's struggles against evil and cheering him on his way.

This is a perennially appealing conception of things. It corresponds to primitive and inveterate tendencies in humanity and gratifies, under the guise of humility, our hungering for self-importance. The mediæval thinker, however freely he might exercise his powers of logical analysis in rationalizing the Christian Epic, never permitted himself to question its general anthropocentric and mystical view of the world. The philosophic mystic assumes the role of a docile child. He feels that all vital truth transcends his powers of discovery. He looks to the Infinite and Eternal Mind to reveal it to him through the prophets of old, or in moments of ecstatic communion with the Divine Intelligence. To the mystic all that concerns our deeper needs transcends logic and defies analysis. In his estimate the human reason is a feeble rushlight which can at best cast a flickering and uncertain ray on the grosser concerns of life, but which only serves to intensify the darkness which surrounds the hidden truth of God.

In order that modern science might develop it is clear that a wholly new and opposed set of fundamental convictions had to be substituted for those of the Middle Ages. Man had to cultivate another kind of self-importance and a new and more profound humility. He had come to believe in his capacity to discover important truth through thoughtful examination of things about him, and he had to recognize, on the other hand, that the world did not seem to be made for him, but that humanity was apparently a curious incident in the universe, and its career a recent episode in cosmic history. He had to acquire a taste for the simplest possible and most thoroughgoing explanation of things. His whole mood had to change and impel him

OUR MEDIÆVAL INHERITANCE

to reduce everything so far as possible to the commonplace.

This new view was inevitably fiercely attacked by the mystically disposed. They misunderstood it and berated its adherents and accused them of robbing man of all that was most precious in life. These, in turn, were goaded into bitterness and denounced their opponents as pig-headed obscurantists.

But we must, after all, come to terms in some way with the emotions underlying mysticism. They are very dear to us, and scientific knowledge will never form an adequate substitute for them. No one need fear that the supply of mystery will ever give out; but a great deal depends on our taste in mystery; that certainly needs refining. What disturbs the so-called rationalist in the mystic's attitude is his propensity to see mysteries where there are none and to fail to see those that we cannot possibly escape. In declaring that one is not a mystic, one makes no claim to be able to explain everything, nor does he maintain that all things are explicable in scientific terms.

Indeed, no thoughtful person will be likely to boast that he can fully explain anything. We have only to scrape the surface of our experiences to find fundamental mystery.

And how, indeed, as descendants of an extinct race of primates, with a mind still in the early stages of accumulation, should we be in the way of reaching ultimate truth at any point? One may properly urge, however, that as sharp a distinction as possible be made between fictitious mysteries and the unavoidable ones which surround us on every side. How milk turned sour used to be a real mystery, now partially solved since the discovery of bacteria; how the witch flew up the chimney was a gratuitous mystery with which we need no longer trouble ourselves. A "live" wire would once have suggested magic; now it is at least partially explained by the doctrine of electrons.

It is the avowed purpose of scientific thought to reduce the number of mysteries, and its success has been marvelous, but it has by no means done its perfect work as yet. We have carried over far too much of mediæval mysticism in our views of man and his duty toward himself and others.

We must now recall the method adopted by students of the natural sciences in breaking away from the standards and limitations of the mediæval philosophers and establishing new standards of their own. They thus prepared the way for a revolution in human affairs in the midst of which we now find ourselves. As yet their type of thinking has not been applied on any considerable scale to the solution of social problems. By learning to understand and appreciate the scientific frame of mind as a historical victory won against extraordinary odds, we may be encouraged to cultivate and popularize a similar attitude toward the study of man himself.

VI

VI

Narrabo igitur primo opera artis et naturæ miranda. . . . ut videatur quod omnis magica potestas sit inferior his operibus et indigna.
—ROGER BACON.

I do not endeavor either by triumphs of confutation, or pleadings of antiquity, or assumption of authority, or even by the veil of obscurity, to invest these inventions of mine with any majesty. . . . I have not sought nor do I seek either to force or ensnare men's judgments, but I lead them to things themselves and the concordances of things, that they may see for themselves what they have, what they can dispute, what they can add and contribute to the common stock.
—FRANCIS BACON (*Preface to the Great Instauration*).

12. THE SCIENTIFIC REVOLUTION

AT the opening of the seventeenth century a man of letters, of sufficient genius to be suspected by some of having written the plays of Shakespeare, directed his distinguished literary ability to the promotion and exaltation of natural science. Lord Bacon was the chief herald of that habit of scientific and critical thought which has played so novel and all-important a part in the making of the modern mind. When but twenty-two years old he was already sketching out a work which he planned to call *Temporis Partus Maximus* (*The Greatest Thing Ever*). He felt that he had discovered why the human mind, enmeshed in mediæval metaphysics and indifferent to natural phenomena, had hitherto been a stunted and ineffective thing, and how it might be so nurtured and guided as to gain undreamed of strength and vigor.

And never has there been a man better equipped with literary gifts to preach a new gospel than Francis Bacon. He spent years in devising eloquent and ingenious ways of delivering learning from the "discredits and disgraces" of the past, and in exhorting man to explore the realms of nature for his delight and profit. He never wearied of trumpeting forth the glories of the new knowledge which would come with the study of common things and the profitable uses to which it might be put in relieving man's estate. He impeached the mediæval schoolmen for spinning out endless cobwebs of learning, remarkable for their fineness, but of no substance or spirit. He urged the learned to come out of their cells, study the creations of God, and build upon what they discovered a new and true philosophy.

Even in his own day students of natural phenomena had begun to carry out Bacon's general program with striking effects. While he was urging men to cease "tumbling up and down in their own reason and conceits" and to spell out, and so by degrees to learn to read, the volume of God's works, Galileo had already begun the reading and had found out that the Aristotelian physics ran counter to the facts; that a body once in motion will continue to move forever in a straight line unless it be stopped or deflected. Studying the sky through his newly invented telescope, he beheld the sun spots and noted the sun's revolution on its axis, the phases of Venus, and the satellites of Jupiter. These discoveries seemed to confirm the ideas advanced long before by Copernicus—the earth was *not* the center of the universe and the heavens were *not* perfect and unchanging. He dared to discuss these matters in the language of the people and was, as everyone knows, condemned by the Inquisition.

This preoccupation with natural phenomena and this refusal to accept the old, established theories until they had been verified by an investigation of common fact was a very novel thing. It introduced a fresh and momentous element into our intellectual heritage. We have recalled the mysticism, supernaturalism, and intolerance of the Middle Ages, their reliance on old books, and their indifference to everyday fact except as a sort of allegory for the edification of the Christian pilgrim. In the mediæval universities the professors, or "schoolmen," devoted themselves to the elaborate formulation of Christian doctrine and the interpretation of Aristotle's works. It was a period of revived Greek metaphysics, adapted to prevailing religious presuppositions. Into this fettered world Bacon, Galileo, Descartes, and others brought a new aspiration to promote investigation and honest, critical thinking about everyday things.

These founders of modern natural science realized that they would have to begin afresh. This was a bold resolve, but not so bold as must be that of the student of mankind to-day if he expects to free himself from the trammels of the past. Bacon pointed out that the old days were not those of mature knowledge, but of youthful human ignorance. "*These* times are the ancient times, when the world is ancient, and not those we count ancient, *ordine retrogrado*, by a computation backward from ourselves." In his *New Atlantis* he pictures an ideal State which concentrated its resources on systematic scientific research, with a view to applying new discoveries to the betterment of man's lot.

Descartes, who was a young man when Bacon was an old one, insisted on the necessity, if we proposed to seek the truth, of questioning *everything* at least once in our lives. To all these leaders in the development of modern science doubt, not faith, was the beginning of wisdom. They doubted—and with good reason—what the Greeks were supposed to have discovered; they doubted all the old books and all the university professors' lecture notes. They did not venture to doubt the Bible, but they eluded it in various ways. They set to work to find out exactly what hap-

THE SCIENTIFIC REVOLUTION

pened under certain circumstances. They experimented individually and reported their discoveries to the scientific academies which began to come into existence.

As one follows the deliberations of these bodies it is pathetic to observe how little the learning of previous centuries, in spite of its imposing claims, had to contribute to a fruitful knowledge of common things. It required a century of hard work to establish the most elementary facts which would now be found in a child's book. How water and air act, how to measure time and temperature and atmospheric pressure, had to be discovered. The microscope revealed the complexity of organic tissues, the existence of minute creatures, vaguely called infusoria, and the strange inhabitants of the blood, the red and white corpuscles. The telescope put an end to the flattering assumption that the cosmos circled around man and the little ball he lives on.

Without a certain un-Greek, practical inventive tendency which, for reasons not easily to be discovered, first began to manifest itself in the thirteenth century, this progress would not have been possible. The new thinkers descended from the magisterial chair and patiently fussed with lenses, tubes, pulleys, and wheels, thus weaning themselves from the adoration of man's mind and understanding. They had to devise the machinery of investigation as investigation itself progressed.

Moreover, they did not confine themselves to the conventionally noble and elevated subjects of speculation. They addressed themselves to worms and ditch water in preference to metaphysical subtleties. They agreed with Bacon that the mean and even filthy things deserve study. All this was naturally scorned by the university professors, and the universities consequently played little or no part in the advance of natural science until the nineteenth century.

Nor were the moral leaders of mankind behind the intellectual in opposing the novel tendencies. The clergy did all they could to perpetuate the squalid belief in witchcraft, but found no place for experimental science in their scheme of learning, and judged it offensive to the Maker of all things. But their opposition could do no more than hamper the new scientific impulse, which was far too potent to be seriously checked.

So in one department of human thought —the investigation of natural processes— majestic progress has been made since the opening of the seventeenth century, with every promise of continued and startling

THE SCIENTIFIC REVOLUTION 157

advance. The new methods employed by students of natural science have resulted in the accumulation of a stupendous mass of information in regard to the material structure and operation of things, and the gradual way in which the earth and all its inhabitants have come into being. The nature and workings of atoms and molecules are being cleared up, and their relation to heat, light, and electricity established. The slow processes which have brought about the mountains and valleys, the seas and plains, have been exposed. The structure of the elementary cell can be studied under powerful lenses; its divisions, conjunctions, differentiation, and multiplication into the incredibly intricate substance of plants and animals can be traced.

In short, man is now in a position, for the first time in his history, to have some really clear and accurate notion of the world in which he dwells and of the living creatures which surround him and with which he must come to terms. It would seem obvious that this fresh knowledge should enable him to direct his affairs more intelligently than his ancestors were able to do in their ignorance. He should be in a position to accommodate himself more and more successfully to the exigencies of an existence which he can understand more fully than any preceding generation, and he should aspire to deal more and more sagaciously with himself and his fellow-men.

13. How Scientific Knowledge Has Revolutionized the Conditions of Life

But while our information in regard to man and the world is incalculably greater than that available a hundred, even fifty years ago, we must frankly admit that the knowledge is still so novel, so imperfectly assimilated, so inadequately co-ordinated, and so feebly and ineffectively presented to the great mass of men, that its *direct* effects upon human impulses and reasoning and outlook are as yet inconsiderable and disappointing. We *might* think in terms of molecules and atoms, but we rarely do. Few have any more knowledge of their own bodily operations than had their grandparents. The farmer's confidence in the phases of the moon gives way but slowly before recent discoveries in regard to the bacteria of the soil. Few who use the telephone, ride on electric cars, and carry a camera have even the mildest curiosity in regard to how these things work. It is only *indirectly*, through *invention*, that scientific knowledge touches our lives on every hand, modifying our environment, altering our daily habits, dislocating the anciently established order, and imposing the burden of constant adaptation on even the most ignorant and lethargic.

Unlike a great part of man's earlier thought, modern scientific knowledge and theory have not remained matter merely for academic discourse and learned books, but have provoked the invention of innumerable practical devices which surround us on every hand, and from which we can now scarce escape by land or sea. Thus while scientific knowledge has not greatly affected the thoughts of most of us, its influence in the promotion of modern invention has served to place us in a new setting or environment, the novel features of which it would be no small task to explain to one's great-great-grandfather, should he unexpectedly apply for up-to-date information. So even if modern scientific *knowledge* is as yet so imperfect and ill understood as to make it impossible for us to apply much of it directly and personally in our daily conduct, we nevertheless cannot neglect the urgent effects of scientific *inventions*, for they are constantly posing new problems of adjustment to us, and sometimes disposing of old ones.

Let us recall a few striking examples of the astonishing way in which what seemed in the beginning to be rather trivial inventions and devices have, with the improvements of modern science, profoundly altered the conditions of life.

Some centuries before the time of Bacon and Galileo four discoveries were made which, supplemented and elaborated by later insight and ingenuity, may be said to underlie our modern civilization. A writer of the time of Henry II of England reports that sailors when caught in fog or darkness were wont to touch a needle to a bit of magnetic iron. The needle would then, it had been found, whirl around in a circle and come to rest pointing north. On this tiny index the vast extension of modern commerce and imperialism rests.

That lentil-shaped bits of glass would magnify objects was known before the end of the thirteenth century, and from that little fact have come microscopes, telescopes, spectroscopes, and cameras; and from these in turn has come a great part of our present knowledge of natural processes in men, animals, and plants and our comprehension of the cosmos at large.

Gunpowder began to be used a few decades

after the lens was discovered; it and its terrible descendants have changed the whole problem of human warfare and of the public defense.

The printing press, originally a homely scheme for saving the labor of the copyist, has not only made modern democracy and nationality possible, but has helped by the extension of education to undermine the ancient foundations upon which human industry has rested from the beginnings of civilization.

In the middle of the eighteenth century the steam engine began to supplant the muscular power of men and animals, which had theretofore been only feebly supplemented by windmills and water wheels. And now we use steam and gas engines and water power to generate potent electric currents which do their work far from the source of supply. Mechanical ingenuity has utilized all this undreamed-of energy in innumerable novel ways for producing old and new commodities in tremendous quantities and distributing them with incredible rapidity throughout the earth.

Vast factories have sprung up, with their laborious multitudes engaged on minute contributions to the finished article; overgrown cities sprawl over the neighboring green fields and pastures; long freight trains of steel cars thunder across continents; monstrous masses of wealth pile up, are reinvested, and applied to making the whole system more and more inconceivably intricate and interdependent; and incidentally there is hurry and worry and discontent and hazard beyond belief for a creature who has to grasp it all and control it all with a mind reared on that of an animal, a child, and a savage.

As if these changes were not astounding enough, now has come the chemist who devotes himself to making not new *commodities* (or old ones in new ways), but new *substances*. He juggles with the atoms of carbon, hydrogen, oxygen, nitrogen, chlorine, and the rest, and far outruns the workings of nature. Up to date he has been able to produce artfully over two hundred thousand compounds, for some of which mankind formerly depended on the alchemy of animals and plants. He can make foodstuffs out of sewage; he can entrap the nitrogen in the air and use it to raise wheat to feed, or high explosives to slaughter, his fellows. He no longer relies on plants and animals for dyes and perfumes. In short, a chemical discovery may at any moment devastate an immemorial industry and leave both capital and labor in the lurch. The day may not be far distant when, should the chemist learn to control the incredible interatomic energy, the steam engine will seem as complete an anachronism as the treadmill.

The uttermost parts of the earth have been visited by Europeans, and commerce has brought all races of the globe into close touch. We have now to reckon with every nation under heaven, as was shown in the World War. At the same time steam and electrical communication have been so perfected that space has been practically annihilated as regards speech, and in matters of transportation reduced to perhaps a fifth. So all the peoples of the earth form economically a loose and, as yet, scarcely acknowledged federation of man, in which the fate of any member may affect the affairs of all the others, no matter how remote they may be geographically.

All these unprecedented conditions have conspired to give business for business' sake a fascination and overwhelming importance it has never had before. We no longer make things for the sake of making them, but for money. The chair is not made to sit on, but for profit; the soap is no longer prepared for purposes of cleanliness, but to be sold for profit. Practically nothing catches our eye in the way of writing that was written for its own sake and not for money. Our magazines and newspapers are our modern commercial travelers proclaiming the gospel of business competition. Formerly the laboring classes worked because they were slaves, or because they were defenseless and could not escape from thraldom—or, mayhap, because they were natural artisans; but now they are coming into a position where they can combine and bargain and enter into business competition with their employers. Like their employers, they are learning to give as little as possible for as much as possible. This is good business; and the employer should realize that at last he has succeeded in teaching his employees to be strictly businesslike. When houses were built to live in, and wheat and cattle grown to eat, these essential industries took care of themselves. But now that profit is the motive for building houses and raising grain, if the promised returns are greater from manufacturing automobiles or embroidered lingerie, one is tempted to ask if there are any longer compelling reasons for building houses or raising food?

Along with the new inventions and discoveries and our inordinately pervasive commerce have come two other novel elements in our environment — what we vaguely call "democracy" and "nationality." These also are to be traced to applied science and mechanical contrivances.

The printing press has made popular education possible, and it is our aspiration to have every boy and girl learn to read and write — an ideal that the Western World has gone far to realize in the last hundred years. General education, introduced first among men and then extended to women, has made plausible the contention that all adults should have a vote, and thereby exercise some ostensible influence in the choice of public officials and in the direction of the policy of the government.

Until recently the mass of the people have not been invited to turn their attention to public affairs, which have been left in the control of the richer classes and their representatives and agents, the statesmen or politicians. Doubtless our crowded cities have contributed to a growing sense of the importance of the common man, for all must now share the street car, the public park, the water supply, and contagious diseases.

But there is a still more fundamental discovery underlying our democratic tendencies. This is the easily demonstrated scientific truth that nearly all men and women, whatever their social and economic status, may have much greater possibilities of activity and thought and emotion than they exhibit in the particular conditions in which they happen to be placed; that in all ranks may be found evidence of unrealized capacity; that we are living on a far lower scale of intelligent conduct and rational enjoyment than is necessary.

Our present notions of nationality are of very recent origin, going back scarcely a hundred years. Formerly nations were made up of the subjects of this or that gracious majesty and were regarded by their God-given rulers as beasts of burden or slaves or, in more amiable moods, as children. The same forces that have given rise to modern democracy have made it possible for vast groups of people, such as make up France or the United States, to be held together more intimately than ever before by the news which reaches them daily of the enterprises of their government and the deeds of their conspicuous fellow-countrymen.

In this way the inhabitants of an extensive territory embracing hundreds of thousands of square miles are brought as close together as the people of Athens in former days. Man is surely a gregarious animal who dislikes solitude. He is, moreover, given to the most exaggerated estimate of his tribe; and on these ancient foundations modern nationality has been built up by means of the printing press, the telegraph, and cheap postage. *So it has fallen out that just when the world was becoming effectively cosmopolitan in its economic interdependence, its scientific research, and its exchange of books and art, the ancient tribal insolence has been developed on a stupendous scale.*

The manner in which man has revolutionized his environment, habits of conduct, and purposes of life by inventions is perhaps the most astonishing thing in human history. It is an obscure and hitherto rather neglected subject. But it is clear enough, from the little that has been said here, that since the Middle Ages, and especially in the past hundred years, science has so hastened the process of change that it becomes increasingly difficult for man's common run of thinking to keep pace with the radical alterations in his actual practices and conditions of living.

12

VII

VII

Peace sitting under her olive, and slurring the days gone by,
When the poor are hovell'd and hustled together, each sex, like swine,
When only the ledger lives, and when only not all men lie;
Peace in her vineyard—yes!—but a company forges the wine.
—Tennyson.

Could great men thunder
As Jove himself does, Jove would ne'er be quiet,
For every pelting, petty officer
Would use his heaven for thunder;
Nothing but thunder!
. . . Man, proud man,
Drest in a little brief authority,
Most ignorant of what he's most assured,
His glassy essence, like an angry ape,
Plays such fantastic tricks before high heaven
As make the angels weep; who, with our spleens,
Would all themselves laugh mortal.
—Shakespeare.

14. "The Sickness of an Acquisitive Society"

IT is so difficult a task to form any correct estimate of one's own surroundings, largely on account of our very familiarity with them, that historical students have generally evaded this responsibility. They have often declared that it was impossible to do so satisfactorily. And yet no one will ever know more than we about what is going on now. Some secrets may be revealed to coming generations, but plenty of our circumstances will be obscure to them. And it certainly seems pusillanimous, if not hazardous, to depute to those yet unborn the task of comprehending the conditions under which we must live and strive. I have long believed that the only unmistakable contribution that the historical student can make to the progress of intelligence is to study the past with an eye constantly on the present. For history not only furnishes us with the key to the present by showing how our situation came about, but at the same time supplies a basis of comparison and a point of vantage by virtue of which the salient contrasts between our days and those of old can be detected. Without history the essential differences are sure to escape us. Our generation, like all preceding generations of mankind, inevitably takes what it finds largely for granted, and the great mass of men who argue about existing conditions assume a fundamental likeness to past conditions as the basis of their conclusions in regard to the present and the still unrolled future.

Such a procedure becomes more and more dangerous, for although a continuity persists, there are more numerous, deeper and wider reaching contrasts between the world of to-day and that of a hundred, or even fifty, years ago, than have developed in any corresponding lapse of time since the beginning of civilization. This is not the place even to sketch the novelties in our knowledge and circumstances, our problems and possibilities. No more can be done here than to illustrate in a single field of human interest the need of an unprecedentedly open mind in order to avail ourselves of existing resources in grasping and manipulating the problems forced upon us.

Few people realize how novel is the almost universal preoccupation with business which we can observe on every hand, but to which we are already so accustomed that it easily escapes the casual observer. But in spite of its vastness and magnificent achievements, business, based upon mass production and speculative profits, has produced new evils and reinforced old ones which no thoughtful person can possibly overlook. Consequently it has become the great issue of our time, the chief subject of discussion, to be defended or attacked according to one's tastes, even as religion and politics formerly had their day.

Business men, whether conspicuous in manufacture, trade, or finance, are the leading figures of our age. They exercise a dominant influence in domestic and foreign policy; they subsidize our education and exert an unmistakable control over it. In other ages a military or religious caste enjoyed a similar pre-eminence. But now business directs and equips the soldier, who is far more dependent on its support than formerly. Most religious institutions make easy terms with business, and, far from interfering with it or its teachings, on the whole cordially support it. Business has its philosophy, which it holds to be based upon the immutable traits of human nature and as identical with morality and patriotism. It is a sensitive, intolerant philosophy, of which something will be said in the following section.

Modern business produced a sort of paradise for the luckier of mankind, which endured down to the war, and which many hope to see restored in its former charm, and perhaps further beautified as the years go on. It represents one of the most startling of human achievements. No doubt a great part of the population worked hard and lived in relative squalor, but even then they had many comforts unknown to the toiling masses of previous centuries, and were apparently fairly contented.

But escape was possible, for any man of capacity or character at all exceeding the average, into the middle or upper classes, for whom life offered, at a low cost and with the least trouble, conveniencies, comforts, and amenities beyond the compass of the richest and most powerful monarchs of other ages. The inhabitant of London could order by telephone, sipping his morning tea in bed, the various products of the whole earth, in such quantity as he might see fit, and reasonably expect their early delivery upon his doorstep; he could at the same moment and by the same means adventure his wealth in the natural resources and new enterprises of any quarter of the world, and share, without exertion or even trouble, in their prospective fruits and advantages. . . . He could secure forthwith, if he wished it, cheap and comfortable means of transit to any country or climate without passport or other formality, could dispatch his servant to the neighboring office of a bank for such supply of the precious metals as might seem convenient, and could then proceed abroad to foreign quarters, without knowledge of their religion, language, or customs, bearing coined wealth upon his person, and would consider himself greatly aggrieved and much surprised at the least interference.

And most important of all, he could, before the war, regard this state of affairs as

> ... normal, certain, and permanent, except in the direction of further improvement, and any deviation from it as aberrant, scandalous, and avoidable. The projects and politics of militarism, and imperialism, of racial and cultural rivalries, of monopolies, restrictions, and exclusion, which were to play the serpent in this paradise, were little more than the amusements of his daily newspaper, and appeared to exercise almost no influence at all on the ordinary course of social and economic life, the internationalization of which was nearly complete in practice.[1]

This assumption of the permanence and normality of the prevailing business system was much disturbed by the outcome of the war, but less so, especially in this country, than might have been expected. It was easy to argue that the terrible conflict merely interrupted the generally beneficent course of affairs which would speedily re-establish itself when given an opportunity. To those who see the situation in this light, modern business has largely solved the age-long problem of producing and distributing the material necessities and amenities of life:

---

[1] Keynes, *The Economic Consequences of the Peace*, pp. 11–12.

and nothing remains except to perfect the system in detail, develop its further potentialities, and fight tooth and nail those who are led by lack of personal success or a maudlin sympathy for the incompetent to attack and undermine it.

On the other hand, there were many before the war, not themselves suffering conspicuously from the system, who challenged its beneficence and permanence, in the name of justice, economy, and the best and highest interests of mankind as a whole. Since the war many more have come to the conclusion that business as now conducted is not merely unfair, exceedingly wasteful, and often highly inexpedient from a social standpoint, but that from an historical standpoint it is "intensely unusual, unstable, complicated, unreliable, and temporary" (Keynes). It may prove to be the chief eccentricity of our age; quite as impermanent as was the feudal and manorial system or the role of the mediæval Church or of monarchs by the grace of God; and destined to undergo changes which it is now quite impossible to forecast.

In any case, economic issues are the chief and bitterest of our time. It is in connection with them that free thinking is most difficult and most apt to be misunderstood, for they easily become confused with the traditional reverences and sanctities of political fidelity, patriotism, morality, and even religion. There is something humiliating about this situation, which subordinates all the varied possibilities of life to its material prerequisites, much as if we were again back in a stage of impotent savagery, scratching for roots and looking for berries and dead animals. One of the most brilliant of recent English economists says with truth:

> The burden of our civilization is not merely, as many suppose, that the product of industry is ill-distributed, or its conduct tyrannical, or its operation interrupted by bitter disagreements. It is that industry itself has come to hold a position of exclusive predominance among human interests, which no single interest, and least of all the provision of the material means of existence, is fit to occupy. Like a hypochondriac who is so absorbed in the processes of his own digestion that he goes to the grave before he has begun to live, industrialized communities neglect the very objects for which it is worth while to acquire riches in their feverish preoccupation with the means by which riches can be acquired.
> That obsession by economic issues is as local and transitory as it is repulsive and disturbing. To future generations it will appear as pitiable as the obsession of the seventeenth century by religious quarrels appears to-day; indeed, it is less rational, since the object with which it is concerned is less important. And it is

a poison which inflames every wound and turns each trivial scratch into a malignant ulcer.[1]

Whatever may be the merits of the conflicting views of our business system, there can be no doubt that it is agitating all types of thoughtful men and women. Poets, dramatists, and story writers turn aside from their old *motifs* to play the role of economists. Psychologists, biologists, chemists, engineers, are as never before striving to discover the relation between their realms of information and the general problems of social and industrial organization. And here is a historical student allowing the dust to collect on mediæval chronicles, church histories, and even seventeenth-century rationalists, once fondly perused, in order to see if he can come to some terms with the profit system. And why not? Are we not all implicated? We all buy and many sell, and no one is left untouched by a situation which can in two or three years halve our incomes, without fault of ours. But before seeking to establish the bearing of the previous sections of this volume

---

[1] Tawney, R. H., *The Acquisitive Society*, pp. 183-184. The original title of this admirable little work, a Fabian tract, was, *The Sickness of an Acquisitive Society*, but the American publishers evidently thought it inexpedient to stress the contention of the author that modern society has anything fundamentally the matter with it.

on our attitude toward the puzzles of our day, we must consider more carefully the "good reasons" commonly urged in defense of the existing system.

15. The Philosophy of Safety and Sanity

So far we have been mainly engaged in recalling the process by which man has accumulated such a mind as he now has, and the effects of this accumulation on his mode of life. Under former conditions (which are now passing away) and in a state of ignorance about highly essential matters (which are now being put in quite a new light) he established certain standards and practices in his political, social, and industrial life. His views of property, government, education, the relations of the sexes, and various other matters he reaffirms and perpetuates by means of schools, colleges, churches, newspapers, and magazines, which in order to be approved and succeed must concur in and ratify these established standards and practices and the current notions of good and evil, right and wrong. This is what happened in the past, and to the great majority of people this still seems to be the only means of "safeguarding society." Before subjecting this attitude of mind to further criticism it will be helpful to see how those argue who fail to perceive the vicious circle involved.

The war brought with it a burst of unwonted and varied animation. Those who had never extended their activities beyond the usual routine of domestic and professional life suddenly found themselves participating in a vast enterprise in which they seemed to be broadening their knowledge and displaying undreamed of capacity for co-operation with their fellows. Expressions of high idealism exalted us above the petty cares of our previous existence, roused new ambitions, and opened up an exhilarating perspective of possibility and endeavor. It was common talk that when the foe, whose criminal lust for power had precipitated the mighty tragedy, should be vanquished, things would "no longer be the same." All would then agree that war was the abomination of abominations, the world would be made safe for right-minded democracy, and the nations would unite in smiling emulation.

Never did bitterer disappointment follow high hopes. All the old habits of nationalistic policy reasserted themselves at Versailles. A frightened and bankrupt world could indeed hardly be expected to exhibit greater intelligence than the relatively happy and orderly one which had five years earlier allowed its sanctified traditions to drag it over the edge of the abyss. Then there emerged from the autocracy of the Tsars the dictatorship of the proletariat, and in Hungary and Germany various startling attempts to revolutionize hastily and excessively that ancient order which the Hapsburg and Hohenzollern rulers had managed to perpetuate in spite of all modern novelties. The real character of these movements was ill understood in our country, but it was inevitable that with man's deep-seated animistic tendencies they should appear as a sort of wicked demon or a deadly contagion which might attack even our own land unless prevented by timely measures. War had naturally produced its machinery for dealing with dissenters, sympathizers with the enemy, and those who deprecated or opposed war altogether; and it was the easiest thing in the world to extend the repression to those who held exceptional or unpopular views, like the Socialists and members of the I. W. W. It was plausible to charge these associations with being under the guidance of foreigners, with "pacifism" and a general tendency to disloyalty. But suspicion went further so as to embrace members of a rather small, thoughtful class who, while rarely socialistic, were confessedly skeptical in regard to the general beneficence of existing institutions, and who failed to applaud at just the right points to suit the taste of the majority of their fellow-citizens. So the general impression grew up that there was a sort of widespread conspiracy to overthrow the government by violence or, at least, a dangerous tendency to prepare the way for such a disaster, or at any rate a culpable indifference to its possibility.

Business depression reinforced a natural reaction which had set in with the sudden and somewhat unexpected close of the war. The unwonted excitement brought on a national headache, and a sedative in the form of normalcy was proffered by the Republican party and thankfully accepted by the country at large. Under these circumstances the philosophy of safety and sanity was formulated. It is familiar and reassuring and puts no disagreeable task of mental and emotional readjustment on those who accept it. Hence its inevitable popularity and obvious soundness.

And these are its presuppositions: No nation is comparable to our own in its wealth and promise, in its freedom and opportunity for all. It has opened its gates to the peoples of the earth, who have flocked across the ocean to escape the poverty and oppression of Europe. From the scattered colonies of the pre-revolutionary period the United States has rapidly advanced to its world ascendancy. When the European powers had reached a hopeless stalemate after four years of war the United States girded on the sword as the champion of liberty and democracy and in an incredibly short time brought the conflict to a victorious close before she had dispatched half the troops she could easily have spared. She had not entered the conflict with any motives of aggrandizement or of territorial extension. She felt her self-sufficiency and could well afford proudly to refuse to join the League of Nations on the ground that she did not wish to be involved in European wrangles or sacrifice a tittle of her rights of self-determination.

The prosperity of the United States is to be attributed largely to the excellence of the Federal Constitution and the soundness of her democratic institutions. Class privileges do not exist, or at least are not recognized. Everyone has equal opportunity to rise in the world unhampered by the shackles of European caste. There is perfect freedom in matters of religious belief. Liberty of speech and of the press is confirmed by both the Federal Constitution and the constitutions of the various states. If people are not satisfied with their form of government they may at any time alter it by a peaceful exercise of the suffrage.

In no other country is morality more highly prized or stoutly defended. Woman is held in her proper esteem and the institution of the family everywhere recognized as fundamental. We are singularly free from the vices which disgrace the capitals of Europe, not excepting London.

In no other country is the schoolhouse so assuredly acknowledged to be the corner stone of democracy and liberty. Our higher institutions of learning are unrivaled; our public libraries numerous and accessible. Our newspapers and magazines disseminate knowledge and rational pleasure throughout the land.

We are an ingenious people in the realm of invention and in the boldness of our business enterprise. We have the sturdy virtues of the pioneer. We are an honest people, keeping our contracts and giving fair measure. We are a tireless people in the patient attention to business and the laudable resolve to rise in the world. Many of our richest men began on the farm or as office boys. Success depends in our

SAFETY AND SANITY

country almost exclusively on native capacity, which is rewarded here with a prompt and cheerful recognition which is rare in other lands.

We are a progressive people, always ready for improvements, which indeed we take for granted, so regularly do they make their appearance. No alert American can visit any foreign country without noting innumerable examples of stupid adherence to outworn and cumbrous methods in industry, commerce, and transportation.

Of course no one is so blind as not to see that here and there evils develop which should be remedied, either by legislation or by the gradual advance in enlightenment. Many of them will doubtless cure themselves. Our democracy is right at heart and you cannot fool all the people all the time. We have not escaped our fair quota of troubles. It would be too much to expect that we should. The difference of opinion between the Northern and Southern states actually led to civil war, but this only served to confirm the natural unity of the country and prepare the way for further advance. Protestants have sometimes dreaded a Catholic domination; the Mormons have been a source of anxiety to timid souls. Populists and advocates of free silver have seemed to threaten sound finance. On the other hand, Wall Street and the trusts have led some to think that corporate business enterprise may at times, if left unhampered, lead to overpowerful monopolies. But the evil workings of all these things had before the war been peaceful, if insidious. They might rouse apprehension in the minds of far-sighted and public-spirited observers, but there had been no general fear that any of them would overthrow the Republic and lead to a violent destruction of society as now constituted and mayhap to a reversion to barbarism.

The circumstances of our participation in the World War and the rise of Bolshevism convinced many for the first time that at last society and the Republic were actually threatened. Heretofore the socialists of various kinds, the communists and anarchists, had attracted relatively little attention in our country. Except for the Chicago anarchist episode and the troubles with the I. W. W., radical reformers had been left to go their way, hold their meetings, and publish their newspapers and pamphlets with no great interference on the part of the police or attention on the part of lawgivers. With the progress of the war this situation changed; police and lawgivers began to interfere, and government

SAFETY AND SANITY

officials and self-appointed guardians of the public weal began to denounce the "reds" and those suspected of "radical tendencies." The report of the Lusk Committee in the state of New York is perhaps the most imposing monument to this form of patriotic zeal.

It is not our business here to discuss the merits of Socialism or Bolshevism either from the standpoint of their underlying theories or their promise in practice. It is only in their effects in developing and subtantiating the philosophy of safety and sanity that they concern us in this discussion.

Whether the report of the so-called Lusk Committee[1] has any considerable influence or no, it well illustrates a common and significant frame of mind and an habitual method of reasoning. The ostensible aim of the report is:

... to give a clear, unbiased statement and history of the purposes and objects, tactics and methods, of the various forces now at work in the United States, and particularly within the state of New York, which are seeking to undermine and destroy, not only the government under which we live, but also the very

---

[1] *Revolutionary Radicalism, Its History, Purpose, and Tactics: with an exposition and discussion of the steps being taken and required to curb it, being the report of the Joint Legislative Committee investigating seditious activities, filed April 24, 1920, in the Senate of the state of New York.* This comprises four stout volumes (over 4,200 pages in all) divided into two parts, dealing, respectively, with "Revolutionary and Subversive Movements at Home and Abroad" and "Constructive Movements and Measures in America." Albany, 1920.

structure of American society. It also seeks to analyze the various constructive forces which are at work throughout the country counteracting these evil influences, and to present the many industrial and social problems that these constructive forces must meet and are meeting.

The plan is executed with laborious comprehensiveness, and one unacquainted with the vast and varied range of so-called "radical" utterances will be overwhelmed by the mass brought together. But our aim here is to consider the attitude of mind and assumptions of the editors and their sympathizers.

They admit the existence of "real grievances and natural demands of the working classes for a larger share in the management and use of the common wealth." It is these grievances and demands which the agitators use as a basis of their machinations. Those bent on a social revolution fall into two classes—socialists and anarchists. But while the groups differ in detail, these details are not worth considering. "Anyone who studies the propaganda of the various groups which we have named will learn that the arguments employed are the same; that the tactics advocated cannot be distinguished from one another, and that articles, or speeches made on the question of tactics or methods by anarchists, could, with propriety, be published in socialist, or communist newspapers without offending the membership of these organizations." So, fortunately for the reader, it is unnecessary to make any distinctions between socialists, anarchists, communists, and Bolsheviki. They all have the common purpose of overthrowing existing society and "general strikes and sabotage are the direct means advocated." The object is to drive business into bankruptcy by reducing production and raising costs.[1]

But it would be a serious mistake to assume that the dangers are confined to our industrial system. "The very first general fact that must be driven home to Americans is that the pacifist movement in this country, the growth and connections of which are an important part of this report, is an absolutely integral and fundamental part of international socialism." European socialism, from which ours is derived, has had for one of its main purposes "the creation of an international sentiment to su-

---

[1] "While the nature of this investigation has led the committee to lay its emphasis upon the activities of subversive organizations, it feels that this report would not be complete if it did not state emphatically that it believes that those persons in business and commercial enterprise and certain owners of property who seek to take advantage of the situation to reap inordinate gain from the public contribute in no small part to the social unrest which affords the radical a field of operation which otherwise would be closed to him." (P. 10.)

persede national patriotism and effort, and this internationalism was based upon pacificism, in the sense that it opposed all wars between nations and developed at the same time class consciousness that was to culminate in relentless class warfare. In other words, it was not really peace that was the goal, but the abolition of the patriotic, warlike spirit of nationalities."

In view of the necessity of making head against this menace the Criminal Anarchy statute of the State of New York was invoked, search warrants issued, "large quantities of revolutionary, incendiary and seditious written and printed matter were seized." After the refusal of Governor Smith to sign them, the so-called Lusk educational bills were repassed and signed by the Republican Governor Miller. No teacher in the schools shall be licensed to teach who "has advocated, either by word of mouth or in writing, a form of government other than the government of the United States or of this state." Moreover, "No person, firm, corporation, association, or society shall conduct, maintain, or operate any school, institute, class, or course of instruction in any subject without making application for and being granted a license from the University of the State of New York [*i. e.* the Regents]."

The Regents shall have the right to send inspectors to visit classes and schools so licensed and to revoke licenses if they deem that an overthrow of the existing government by violence is being taught.[1]

But the safe and sane philosophy by no means stops with the convenient and compendious identification of socialists of all kinds, anarchists, pacificists and internationalists, as belonging to one threatening group united in a like-minded attempt to overthrow society as we now know it. This class includes, it may be observed, such seemingly distinguishable personalities as Trotzky and Miss Jane Addams, who are assumed to be in essential harmony upon the great issue. But there are many others who are perhaps the innocent tools of the socialists. These include teachers, lecturers, writers, clergymen, and editors to whom the Lusk report devotes a long section on "the spread of socialism in educated circles." It is the purpose of this section

... to show the use made by members of the Socialist Party of America and other extreme radicals and revolutionaries of pacifist sentiment among people of education and culture in the United States as a vehicle

---

[1] The general history throughout the United States of these and similar measures, the interference with public meetings, the trials, imprisonments, and censorship, are all set forth in Professor Chaffee's *Freedom of Speech*, 1920.

for the promotion of revolutionary socialistic propaganda. The facts here related are important because they show that these socialists, playing upon the pacifist sentiment in a large body of sincere persons, were able to organize their energies and capitalize their prestige for the spread of their doctrines. [P. 969.]

An instance of this is an article in the *New Republic* which

... includes more or less open attacks on Attorney-General Palmer, Mr. Lansing, the House Immigration Committee, the New York *Times*, Senator Fall, this Committee, etc. It also quotes the dissenting opinions in the Abrams case of Justices Holmes and Brandeis, and ends by making light of the danger of revolution in America: ... This belittling of the very real danger to the institutions of this country, as well as the attempted discrediting of any investigating group (or individual), has become thoroughly characteristic of our "Parlor Bolshevik" or "Intelligentsia." [P. 1103.]

So it comes about, as might indeed have been foreseen from the first, that one finds himself, if not actually violating the criminal anarchy statute, at least branded as a Bolshevik if he speaks slightingly of the New York *Times* or recalls the dissenting opinion of two judges of the Supreme Court.

Moreover, as might have been anticipated, the issues prove to be at bottom not so much economic as moral and religious, for "Materialism and its formidable sons, Anarchy,

Bolshevism, and Unrest, have thrown down the gauge of battle" to all decency.

... What is of the greatest importance for churchmen to understand, in order that they may not be led astray by specious arguments of so-called Christian Socialists and so-called liberals and self-styled partisans of free speech, is that socialism as a system, as well as anarchism and all its ramifications, from high-brow Bolshevism to the Russian Anarchist Association, are all the declared enemies of religion and all recognized moral standards and restraints. [P. 1124.]

We must not be misled by "false, specious idealism masquerading as progress." The fight is one for God as well as country, in which all forms of radicalism, materialism, and anarchy should be fiercely and promptly stamped out.[1]

[1] During the summer of 1921 the Vice-President of the United States published in *The Delineator* a series of three articles on "Enemies of the Republic," in which he considers the question, "Are the 'reds' stalking our college women?" He finds some indications that they are, and warns his readers that, "Adherence to radical doctrines means the ultimate breaking down of the old, sturdy virtues of manhood and womanhood, the insidious destruction of character, the weakening of the moral fiber of the individual, and the destruction of the foundations of society." It may seem anomalous to some that the defenders of the old, sturdy virtues should so carelessly brand honest and thoughtful men and women, of whose opinions they can have no real knowledge, as "enemies of the Republic"—but there is nothing whatever anomalous in this. It has been the habit of defenders of the sturdy, old virtues from time immemorial to be careless of others' reputations.

VIII

VIII

Dans les sciences politiques, il est un ordre de vérités qui, surtout chez les peuples libres ... ne peuvent être utiles, que lorsqu'elles sont généralement connues et avouées. Ainsi, l'influence du progrès de ces sciences sur la liberté, sur la prospérité des nations, doivent en quelque sorts se mesurer sur le nombre de ces vérités qui, par l'effet d'une instruction élémentaire, deviennent commune à tous les esprits; ainsi les progrès toujours croissants de cette instruction élémentaire, liés eux mêmes aux progrès nécessaires de ces sciences, nous répondent d'une amélioration dans les destinées de l'espèce humaine qui peut être regardé ecomme indéfinie, puisqu'elle n'a d'autres limites que celles de ces progrès mêmes.—CONDORCET.

16. Some Historical Reflections on the Philosophy of Repression

OF course the kind of reasoning and the presuppositions described in the previous section will appeal to many readers as an illustration of excessive and unjustifiable fear lest the present order be disturbed—a frenzied impulse to rush to the defense of our threatened institutions. Doubtless the Lusk report may quite properly be classed as a mere episode in war psychology. Having armed to put down the Germans and succeeded in so doing, the ardor of conflict does not immediately abate, but new enemies are sought and easily discovered. The hysteria of repression will probably subside, but it is now a well-recognized fact that in disease, whether organic or mental, the abnormal and excessive are but instructive exaggerations and perversions of the usual course of things. They do not exist by themselves, but represent the temporary and exaggerated functioning of bodily and mental processes. The real question for us here is not whether Senator Lusk is too fearful and too indiscriminate in his denunciations, but whether he and his colleagues do not merely furnish an overcharged and perhaps somewhat grotesque instance of man's natural and impulsive way of dealing with social problems. It seems to me that enough has already been said to lead us to suspect this.

At the outset of this volume the statement was hazarded that if only men could come to look at things differently from the way they now generally do, a number of our most shocking evils would either remedy themselves or show themselves subject to gradual elimination or hopeful reduction. Among these evils a very fundamental one is the defensive attitude toward the criticism of our existing order and the naïve tendency to class critics as enemies of society. It was argued that a fuller understanding of the history of the race would contribute to that essential freedom of mind which would welcome criticism and permit fair judgments of its merits. Having reviewed the arguments of those who would suppress criticism lest it lead to violence and destruction, we may now properly recall in this connection certain often neglected historical facts which serve to weaken if not to discredit most of these arguments.

Man has never been able to adapt himself

very perfectly to his civilization, and there has always been a deal of injustice and maladjustment which might conceivably have been greatly decreased by intelligence. But now it would seem that this chronic distress has become acute, and some careful observers express the quite honest conviction that unless thought be raised to a far higher plane than hitherto, some great setback to civilization is inevitable.

Yet instead of subjecting traditional ideas and rules to a thoroughgoing reconsideration, our impulse is, as we have seen, to hasten to justify existing and habitual notions of human conduct. There are many who flatter themselves that by suppressing so-called "radical" thought and its diffusion, the present system can be made to work satisfactorily on the basis of ideas of a hundred or a hundred thousand years ago.

While we have permitted our free thought in the natural sciences to transform man's old world, we allow our schools and even our universities to continue to inculcate beliefs and ideals which may or may not have been appropriate to the past, but which are clearly anachronisms now. For, the "social science" taught in our schools is, it would appear, an orderly presentation of the conventional proprieties, rather than a summons to grapple with the novel and disconcerting facts that surround us on every side.

At the opening of the twentieth century the so-called sciences of man, despite some progress, are, as has been pointed out, in much the same position that the natural sciences were some centuries earlier. Hobbes says of the scholastic philosophy that it went on one brazen leg and one of an ass. This seems to be our plight to-day. Our scientific leg is lusty and grows in strength daily; its fellow member —our thought of man and his sorry estate—is capricious and halting. We have not realized the hopes of the eighteenth-century "illumination," when confident philosophers believed that humanity was shaking off its ancient chains; that the clouds of superstition were lifting, and that with the new achievements of science man would boldly and rapidly advance toward hitherto undreamed-of concord and happiness. We can no longer countenance the specious precision of the English classical school of economics, whose premises have been given the lie by further thought and experience. We have really to start anew.

The students of natural phenomena early realized the arduous path they had to travel. They had to escape, above all things, from the past. They perceived that they could look for no help from those whose special business it was to philosophize and moralize in terms of the past. They had to look for light in their own way and in the directions from which they conjectured it might come. Their first object was, as Bacon put it, *light*, not *fruit*. They had to learn before they could undertake changes, and Descartes is very careful to say that philosophic doubt was not to be carried over to daily conduct. This should for the time being conform to accepted standards, unenlightened as they might be.

Such should be the frame of mind of one who seeks insight into human affairs. His subject matter is, however, far more intricate and unmanageable than that of the natural scientist. Experiment on which natural science has reared itself is by no means so readily applicable in studying mankind and its problems. The student of humanity has even more inveterate prejudices to overcome, more inherent and cultivated weaknesses of the mind to guard against, than the student of nature. Like the early scientists, he has a scholastic tradition to combat. He can look for little help from the universities as now constituted. The clergy, although less sensitive in regard to what they find in the Bible, are still stoutly opposed, on the whole, to any thoroughgoing criticism of the standards of morality to which they are accustomed. Few lawyers can view their profession with any considerable degree of detachment. Then there are the now all-potent business interests, backed by the politicians and in general supported by the ecclesiastical, legal, and educational classes. Many of the newspapers and magazines are under their influence, since they are become the business man's heralds and live off his bounty.

Business indeed has almost become our religion; it is defended by the civil government even as the later Roman emperors and the mediæval princes protected the Church against attack. Socialists and communists are the Waldensians and Albigensians of our day, heretics to be cast out, suppressed, and deported to Russia, if not directly to hell as of old.

The Secret Service seems inclined to play the part of a modern Inquisition, which protects our new religion. Collected in its innumerable files is the evidence in regard to suspected heretics who have dared impugn "business as usual," or who have dwelt too lovingly on peace and good will among nations. Books and pamphlets, although no longer burned by the common hangman, are forbidden the mails by somewhat undiscerning officials. We have a pious vocabulary of high resentment and noble condemnation, even as they had in the Middle Ages, and part of it is genuine, if unintelligent, as it was then.

Such are some of the obstacles which the student of human affairs must surmount. Yet we may hope that it will become increasingly clear that the repression of criticism (even if such criticism becomes fault-finding and takes the form of a denunciation of existing habits and institutions) is inexpedient and inappropriate to the situation in which the world finds itself. Let us assume that such people as really advocate lawlessness and disorder should be carefully watched and checked if they promise to be a cause of violence and destruction. But is it not possible to distinguish between them and those who question and even arraign with some degree of heat the standardized unfairness and maladjustments of our times?

And there is another class who cannot by any exaggeration be considered agitators, who have by taking thought come to see that our conditions have so altered in the past hundred years and our knowledge so increased that the older ways of doing and viewing things are not only unreasonable, but actually dangerous. But so greatly has the hysteria of war unsettled the public mind that even this latter class is subject to discreditable accusations and some degree of interference.

We constantly hear it charged that this or that individual or group advocates the violent overthrow of government, is not loyal to the Constitution, or is openly or secretly working for the abolition of private property or the family, or, in general, is supposed to be eager to "overturn everything without having anything to put in its place."

The historical student may well recommend that we be on our guard against such accusations brought against groups and individuals. For the student of history finds that it has always been the custom to charge those who happened to be unpopular, with holding beliefs and doing things which they neither believed nor did. Socrates was executed for corrupting youth and infidelity to the gods; Jesus for proposing to overthrow the government; Luther was to the officials of his time one who taught "a loose, self-willed life, severed from all laws and wholly brutish."

Those who questioned the popular delusions in regard to witchcraft were declared by clergymen, professors, and judges of the seventeenth century to be as good as atheists, who shed doubt on the devil's existence in order to lead their godless lives without fear of future retribution. How is it possible, in view of this inveterate habit of mankind, to accept at its face value what the police or Department of Justice, or self-appointed investigators, choose to report of the teachings of people who are already condemned in their eyes?

Of course the criticism of accepted ideas is offensive and will long remain so. After all, talk and writing are forms of conduct, and, like all conduct, are inevitably disagreeable when they depart from the current standards of respectable behavior. To talk as if our established notions of religion, morality, and property, our ideas of stealing and killing, were defective and in need of revision, is indeed more shocking than to violate the current rules of action. For we are accustomed to actual crimes, misdemeanors, and sins, which are happening all the time, but we will not tolerate any suspected attempt to palliate them in theory.

It is inevitable that new views should appear to the thoughtless to be justifications or extenuations of evil actions and an encouragement of violence and rebellion, and that they will accordingly be bitterly denounced. But there is no reason why an increase of intelligence should not put a growing number of us on our guard against this ancient pitfall.

If we are courageously to meet and successfully to overcome the dangers with which our civilization is threatened, it is clear that we need *more mind* than ever before. It is also clear that we can have indefinitely more mind than we already have if we but honestly desire it and avail ourselves of resources already at hand. Mind, as previously defined, is our "conscious knowledge and intelligence, what we know and our attitude toward it— our disposition to increase our information, classify it, criticize it, and apply it." *It is obvious that in this sense the mind is a matter of accumulation and that it has been in the making ever since man took his first step in civilization.* I have tried to suggest the manner in which man's long history illuminates our plight and casts light on the path to be followed. And history is beginning to take account of the knowledge of man's nature and origin contributed by the biologist and the anthropologist and the newer psychologists.

PHILOSOPHY OF REPRESSION

Few people realize the hopeful revolution that is already beginning to influence the aims and methods of all these sciences of man. No previous generation of thinkers has been so humble on the whole as is that of to-day, so ready to avow their ignorance and to recognize the tendency of each new discovery to reveal further complexities in the problem. On the other hand, we are justified in feeling that at last we have the chance to start afresh. We are freer than any previous age from the various prepossessions and prejudices which we now see hampered the so-called "free" thinking of the eighteenth century.

The standards and mood of natural science are having an increasing influence in stimulating eager research into human nature, beliefs, and institutions. With Bacon's recommendations of the study of common *things* the human mind entered a new stage of development. Now that historic forces have brought the common *man* to the fore, we are submitting him to scientific study and gaining thereby that elementary knowledge of his nature which needs to be vastly increased and spread abroad, since it can form the only possible basis for a successful and real democracy.

I would not have the reader infer that I overrate the place of science or exact knowledge in the life of man. Science, which is but the most accurate information available about the world in which we live and the nature of ourselves and of our fellow men, is not the whole of life; and except to a few peculiar persons it can never be the most absorbing and vivid of our emotional satisfactions. We are poetic and artistic and romantic and mystical. We resent the cold analysis and reduction of life to the commonplace and well substantiated—and this is after all is said, the aim of scientific endeavor. But we have to adjust ourselves to a changing world in the light of constantly accumulating knowledge. It is knowledge that has altered the world and we must rely on knowledge and understanding to accommodate ourselves to our new surroundings and establish peace and order and security for the pursuit of those things that to most of us are more enticing than science itself.[1]

---

[1] Mr. James Branch Cabell has in his *Beyond Life* defended man's romantic longings and inexorable craving to live part of the time at least in a world far more sweetly molded to his fancy than that of natural science and political economy. There is no reason why man should live by bread alone. There is a time, however, for natural science and political economy, for they should establish the conditions in which we may rejoice in our vital lies, which will then do no harm and bring much joy.

PHILOSOPHY OF REPRESSION

No previous generation has been so perplexed as ours, but none has ever been justified in holding higher hopes if it could but reconcile itself to making bold and judicious use of its growing resources, material and intellectual. *It is fear that holds us back.* And fear is begotten of ignorance and uncertainty. And these mutually reinforce one another, for we feebly try to condone our ignorance by our uncertainty and to excuse our uncertainty by our ignorance.

Our hot defense of our ideas and beliefs does not indicate an established confidence in them but often half-distrust, which we try to hide from ourselves, just as one who suffers from bashfulness offsets his sense of inferiority and awkwardness by rude aggression. If, for example, religious beliefs had been really firmly established there would have been no need of "aids to faith"; and so with our business system to-day, our politics and international relations. We dread to see things as they would appear if we thought of them honestly, for it is the nature of critical thought to metamorphose our familiar and approved world into something strange and unfamiliar. It is undoubtedly a nervous sense of the precariousness of the existing social system which accounts for the present strenuous opposition to a fair and square consideration of irs merits and defects.

Partisanship is our great curse. We too readily assume that everything has two sides and that it is our duty to be on one or the other. We must be defending or attacking something; only the lily-livered hide their natural cowardice by asking the impudent question, What is it all about? The heroic gird on the armor of the Lord, square their shoulders, and establish a muscular tension which serves to dispel doubt and begets the voluptuousness of bigotry and fanaticism.[1] In this mood questions become issues of right and wrong, not of expediency and inexpediency. It has been said that the worthy people of Cambridge are able promptly to reduce the most complex social or economic problem to a simple moral issue, and this is a wile of the Father of Lies, to which many of us yield readily enough.

It is, however, possible for the individual to overcome the fear of thought. Once I was afraid that men might think too much; now, I only dread lest they will think too little and far too timidly, for I now see that real thinking

---

[1] The relation of our kinesthesia or muscular sense to fanaticism on the one hand and freedom of mind on the other is a matter now beginning to be studied with the promise of highly important results.

is rare and difficult and that it needs every incentive in the face of innumerable ancient and inherent discouragements and impediments. We must first endeavor manfully to free our own minds and then do what we can to hearten others to free theirs. *Toujours de l'audace!* As members of a race that has required from five hundred thousand to a million years to reach its present state of enlightenment, there is little reason to think that anyone of us is likely to cultivate intelligence too assiduously or in harmful excess.

17. What of It?

Our age is one of unprecedented responsibility. As Mr. Lippmann has so well said:

Never before have we had to rely so completely on ourselves. No guardian to think for us, no precedent to follow without question, no lawmaker above, only ordinary men set to deal with heartbreaking perplexity. All weakness comes to the surface. We are homeless in a jungle of machines and untamed powers that haunt and lure the imagination. Of course our culture is confused, our thinking spasmodic, and our emotion out of kilter. No mariner ever enters upon a more uncharted sea than does the average human being born in the twentieth century. Our ancestors thought they knew their way from birth through all eternity; we are puzzled about day after to-morrow. . . . It is with emancipation that real tasks begin, and liberty is a searching challenge, for it takes away the guardianship of the master and the comfort of the priest. The iconoclasts did not free us. They threw us into the water, and now we have to swim.[1]

We must look forward to ever new predicaments and adventures. *Nothing is going to be settled in the sense in which things were once supposed to be settled, for the simple reason that knowledge will probably continue to increase and will inevitably alter the world with which we have to make terms.* The only thing that might conceivably remain somewhat stabilized is an attitude of mind and unflagging expectancy appropriate to the terms and the rules according to which life's game must hereafter be played. We must promote a new cohesion and co-operation on the basis of this truth. And this means that we have now to substitute purpose for tradition, and this is a concise statement of the great revolution which we face.

Now, when all human institutions so slowly and laboriously evolved are impugned, every consensus challenged, every creed flouted, as much as and perhaps even more than by the ancient Sophists, the call comes to us . . . to explore, test, and, if necessary, reconstruct the very bases of conviction, for all open questions are new opportunities. Old beacon lights have shifted or gone out. Some of the issues we lately thought to be minor have taken on cosmic dimensions. We are all "up against" questions too big for us, so that there is everywhere a sense of insufficiency which

[1] *Drift and Mastery*, pp. 196–197.

is too deep to be fully deployed in the narrow field of consciousness. Hence, there is a new discontent with old leaders, standards, criteria, methods, and values, and a demand everywhere for new ones, a realization that mankind must now reorient itself and take its bearings from the eternal stars and sail no longer into the unknown future by the dead reckonings of the past.[1]

Life, in short, has become a solemn sporting proposition—solemn enough in its heavy responsibilities and the magnitude of the stakes to satisfy our deepest religious longings; sporty enough to tickle the fancy of a baseball fan or an explorer in darkest Borneo. We can play the game or refuse to play it. At present most of human organization, governmental, educational, social, and religious, is directed, as it always has been, to holding things down, and to perpetuating beliefs and policies which belong to the past and have been but too gingerly readjusted to our new knowledge and new conditions. On the other hand, there are various scientific associations which are bent on revising and amplifying our knowledge and are not pledged to keeping alive any belief or method which cannot stand the criticism which comes with further information. The terrible fear of falling into mere rationalizing

---

[1] G. Stanley Hall, "The Message of the Zeitgeist," in *Scientific Monthly*, August, 1921—a very wonderful and eloquent appeal by one of our oldest and boldest truth seekers.

is gradually extending from the so-called natural sciences to psychology, anthropology, politics, and political economy. All this is a cheering response to the new situation.

But, as has been pointed out, really honest discussion of our social, economic, and political standards and habits readily takes on the suspicion of heresy and infidelity. Just as the "freethinker" who, in the eighteenth century, strove to discredit miracles in the name of an all-wise and foreseeing God (who could not be suspected of tampering with his own laws), was accused of being an atheist and of really believing in no God at all; so those who would ennoble our ideals of social organization are described as "Intellectuals" or "parlor Bolshevists" who would overthrow society and all the achievements of the past in order to free themselves from moral and religious restraints and mayhap "get something for nothing." The parallel is very exact indeed.

The Church always argued that there were no new heresies. All would, on examination, prove to be old and discredited. So the Vice-President of the United States has recently declared that:

> Men have experimented with radical theories in great and small ways times without number and always, always with complete failure. They are not

WHAT OF IT? 215

new; they are old. Each failure has demonstrated anew that without effort there is no success. The race never gets something for nothing.[1]

But is this not a complete reversal of the obvious truth? Unless we define "radical" as that which never does succeed, how can anyone with the most elementary notions of history fail to see that almost all the things that we prize to-day represent revolts against tradition, and were in their beginnings what seemed to be shocking divergences from current beliefs and practices? What about Christianity, and Protestantism, and constitutional government, and the rejection of old superstitions and the acceptance of modern scientific ideas? The race has always been getting something for nothing, for creative thought is, as we have seen, confined to a very few. And it has been the custom to discourage or kill those who prosecuted it too openly, not to reward them according to their merits.

One cannot but wonder at this constantly recurring phrase "getting something for nothing," as if it were the peculiar and perverse ambition of disturbers of society. Except for our animal outfit, practically all we have is handed to us gratis. Can the most complacent reactionary flatter himself that he

---
[1] *Delineator*, August, 1921, p. 11.

invented the art of writing or the printing press, or discovered his religious, economic, and moral convictions, or any of the devices which supply him with meat and raiment or any of the sources of such pleasure as he may derive from literature or the fine arts? In short, civilization is little else than getting something for nothing. Like other vested interests, it is "the legitimate right to something for nothing."[1] How much execrable reasoning and how many stupid accusations would fall away if this truth were accepted as a basis of discussion! Of course there is no more flagrant example of a systematic endeavor to get something for nothing than the present business system based on profits, and absentee ownership of stocks.

Since the invention of printing, and indeed long before, those fearful of change have attempted to check criticism by attacking books. These were classified as orthodox or heterodox, moral or immoral, treasonable or loyal, according to their tone. Unhappily this habit continues and shows itself in the distinction between sound and unsound, radical and conservative, safe and dangerous.

---

[1] Adopting Mr. Veblen's definition of a vested interest which caused some scandal in conservative circles when it was first reported. Doubtless the seeming offensiveness of the latter part of the definition obscured its reassuring beginning.

WHAT OF IT?

The sensible question to ask about a book is obviously whether it makes some contribution to a clearer understanding of our situation by adding or reaffirming important considerations and the inferences to be made from these. Such books could be set off against those that were but expressions of vague discontent or emulation, or denunciations of things because they are as they are or are not as they are not. I have personally little confidence in those who cry lo here or lo there. It is premature to advocate any wide sweeping reconstruction of the social order, although experiments and suggestions should not be discouraged. What we need first is a change of heart and a chastened mood which will permit an ever increasing number of people to see things as they are, in the light of what they have been and what they might be. The dogmatic socialist with his unhistorical assumptions of class struggle, his exaggerated economic interpretation of history, and his notion that labor is the sole producer of capital, is shedding scarcely more light on the actual situation than is the Lusk Committee and Mr. Coolidge, with their confidence in the sacredness of private property, as they conceive it, in the perennial rightness and inspiration of existing authority and the blessedness of the profit system. But there are plenty of writers, to mention only a few of the more recent ones, like Veblen, Dewey, J. A. Hobson, Tawney, Cole, Havelock Ellis, Bertrand Russell, Graham Wallas, who may or may not have (or ever have had) any confidence in the presuppositions and forecasts of socialism, whose books do make clearer to any fair-minded reader the painful exigencies of our own times.

I often think of the economic historians of, say, two centuries hence who may find time to dig up the vestiges of the economic literature of to-day. We may in imagination appeal to their verdicts and in some cases venture to forecast them. Many of our writers they will throw aside as dominated by a desire merely to save the ill-understood present at all costs; others as attempting to realize plans which were already discredited in their own day. Future historians will, nevertheless, clearly distinguish a few who, by a sort of persistent and ardent detachment, were able to see things close at hand more fully and truly than their fellows and endeavored to do what they could to lead their fellows to perceive and reckon with the facts which so deeply concerned them. Blessed be those who aspire to win this glory. On the monument erected to Bruno on the site where he was burned for seeing more clearly than those in authority in his days, is the simple inscription, "Raised to Giordano Bruno by the generation which he foresaw."

We are all purblind, but some are blinder than others who use the various means available for sharpening their eyesight. As an onlooker it seems to me safe to say that the lenses recommended by both the "radicals" and their vivid opponents rather tend to increase than diminish our natural astigmatism.

Those who agree, on the whole, at least, with the *facts* brought together in this essay and, on the whole, with the main *inferences* suggested either explicitly or implicitly, will properly begin to wonder how our educational system and aims are to be so rearranged that coming generations may be better prepared to understand the condition of human life and to avail themselves of its possibilities more fully and guard against its dangers more skillfully than previous generations. There is now widespread discontent with our present educational methods and their elaborate futility; but it seems to me that we are rather rarely willing to face the fundamental difficulty, for it is obviously so very hard to overcome. *We do not dare to be honest enough to tell boys and girls and young men and women what would be most useful to them in an age of imperative social reconstruction.*

We have seen that the ostensible aims of education are various,[1] and that among them is now included the avowed attempt to prepare the young to play their part later as voting citizens. If they are to do better than preceding generations they must be brought up differently. They would have to be given a different general attitude toward institutions and ideals; instead of having these represented to them as standardized and sacred they should be taught to view them as representing half-solved problems. But how can we ever expect to cultivate the judgment of the young in matters of fundamental social, economic, and political readjustment when we consider the really dominating forces in education? But even if these restraints were weakened or removed, the task would remain a very delicate one. Even with teachers free and far better informed than they are, it would be no easy thing to cultivate in the young a justifiable admiration for the achievements and traditional ideals of man-

---
[1] See Section 2 above.

kind and at the same time develop the requisite knowledge of the prevailing abuses, culpable stupidity, common dishonesty, and empty political buncombe, which too often passes for statesmanship.

But the problem has to be tackled, and it may be tackled directly or indirectly. The direct way would be to describe as realistically as might be the actual conditions and methods, and their workings, good and bad. If there were better books than are now available it would be possible for teachers tactfully to show not only how government is supposed to run, but how it actually is run. There are plenty of reports of investigating committees, Federal and state, which furnish authentic information in regard to political corruption, graft, waste, and incompetency. These have not hitherto been supposed to have anything to do with the *science* of government, although they are obviously absolutely essential to an *understanding* of it. Similar reflections suggest themselves in the matter of business, international relations, and race animosities. But so long as our schools depend on appropriations made by politicians, and colleges and universities are largely supported by business men or by the state, and are under the control of those who are bent on preserving the existing system from criticism, it is hard to see any hope of a kind of education which would effectively question the conventional notions of government and business. They cannot be discussed with sufficient honesty to make their consideration really medicinal. We laud the brave and outspoken and those supposed to have the courage of their convictions—but only when these convictions are acceptable or indifferent to us. Otherwise, honesty and frankness become mere impudence.[1]

No doubt politics and economics could be taught, and are being taught, better as time goes on. Neither of them are so utterly unreal and irrelevant to human proceedings as they formerly were. There is no reason why a teacher of political economy should not describe the actual workings of the profit system of industry with its restraints on production and its dependence on the engineer, and suggest the possibility of gathering together capital from functionless absentee stockholders on the basis of the current rate of interest rather than speculative dividends. The actual conditions of the workers could be

---

[1] The wise Goethe has said, "*Zieret Stärke den Mann und freies, muthiges Wesen, O, so ziemet ihm fast tiefes Geheimniss noch mehr.*" —*Römische Elegien*, xx.

described, their present precarious state, the inordinate and wasteful prevalence of hiring and firing; the policy of the unions, and their defensive and offensive tactics. Every youngster might be given some glimmering notion that neither "private property" nor "capital" is the real issue (since few question their essentiality) but rather the new problem of supplying other than the traditional motives for industrial enterprise—namely, the slave-like docility and hard compulsion of the great masses of workers, on the one hand, and speculative profits, on the other, which now dominate in our present business system. For the existing organization is not only becoming more and more patently wasteful, heartless, and unjust, but is beginning, for various reasons, to break down. In short, whatever the merits of our present ways of producing the material necessities and amenities of life, it looks to many as if they could not succeed indefinitely, even as well as they have in the past, without some fundamental revision.

As for political life, a good deal would be accomplished if students could be habituated to distinguish successfully between the empty declamations of politicians and statements of facts, between vague party programs and concrete recommendations and proposals. They should early learn that language is not primarily a vehicle of ideas and information, but an emotional outlet, corresponding to various cooings, growlings, snarls, crowings, and brayings. Their attention could be invited to the rhetoric of the bitter-enders in the Senate or the soothing utterances of Mr. Harding on accepting the nomination for President:

"With a Senate advising as the Constitution contemplates, I would hopefully approach the nations of Europe and of the earth, proposing that understanding which makes us a willing participant in the consecration of nations to a new relationship, to commit the moral forces of the world, America included, to peace and international justice, still leaving America free, independent, self-reliant, but offering friendship to all the world. If men call for more specific details, I remind them that moral committals are broad and all-inclusive, and we are contemplating peoples in the concord of humanity's advancement."

After mastering the difference between language used to express facts and purposes and that which amounts to no more than a pious ejaculation, a suave and deprecating gesture, or an inferential accusation directed against the opposing party, the youth should be instructed in the theory and practice of party fidelity and the effects of partisanship on the conduct of our governmental affairs. In fine, he should get some notion of the motives and methods of those who really run our government, whether he learned anything else or not.

These *direct* attempts to produce a more intelligently critical and open-minded generation are, however, likely to be far less feasible than the *indirect* methods. Partly because they will arouse strenuous opposition from the self-appointed defenders of society as now regulated, and partly because no immediate inspection of habits and institutions is so instructive as a study of their origin and progress and a comparison of them with other forms of social adjustment. I hope that it has already become clear that we have great, and hitherto only very superficially worked, resources in History, as it is now coming to be conceived.

We are in the midst of the greatest intellectual revolution that has ever overtaken mankind. Our whole conception of mind is undergoing a great change. We are beginning to understand its nature, and as we find out more, intelligence may be raised to a recognized dignity and effectiveness which it has never enjoyed before. An encouraging beginning has been made in the case of the natural sciences, and a similar success may await the studies which have to do with the critical estimate of man's complicated nature, his fundamental impulses and resources, the needless and fatal repressions which these have suffered through the ignorance of the past, and the discovery of untried ways of enriching our existence and improving our relations with our fellow men.

There[1] is a well-known passage in Goethe's "Faust" where he likens History to the Book with Seven Seals described in Revelation, which no one in heaven, or on the earth or under the earth, was able to open and read therein. All sorts of guesses have been hazarded as to its contents by Augustine, Orosius, Otto of Freising, Bossuet, Bolingbroke, Voltaire, Herder, Hegel, and many others, but none of them were able to break the seals, and all of them were gravely misled by their fragmentary knowledge of the book's contents. For we now see that the seven seals were seven great ignorances. No one knew much (1) of man's physical nature, or (2) the workings of his thoughts and desires, or (3) of the world

---

[1] The closing reflections are borrowed from *The Leaflet*, issued by the students of the New School for Social Research, established in New York in 1919, with a view of encouraging adults to continue their studies in the general spirit and mood which permeate this essay.

in which he lives, or (4) of how he has come about as a race, or (5) of how he develops as an individual from a tiny egg, or (6) how deeply and permanently he is affected by the often forgotten impressions of infancy and childhood, or (7) how his ancestors lived for hundreds of thousands of years in the dark ignorance of savagery.

The seals are all off now. The book at last lies open before those who are capable of reading it, and few they be as yet; for most of us still cling to the guesses made in regard to its contents before anyone knew what was in it. We have become attached to the familiar old stories which now prove to be fictions, and we find it hard to reconcile ourselves to the many hard sayings which the book proves to contain—its constant stress on the stupidity of "good" people; its scorn for the respectable and normal, which it often reduces to little more than sanctimonious routine and indolence and pious resentment at being disturbed in one's complacent assurances. Indeed, much of its teaching appears downright immoral according to existing standards.

One awful thing that the Book of the Past makes plain is that with our animal heritage we are singularly oblivious to the large concerns of life. We are keenly sensitive to little discomforts, minor irritations, wounded vanity, and various danger signals; but our comprehension is inherently vague and listless when it comes to grasping intricate situations and establishing anything like a fair perspective in life's problems and possibilities. Our imagination is restrained by our own timidity, constantly reinforced by the warnings of our fellows, who are always urging us to be safe and sane, by which they mean convenient for them, predictable in our conduct and graciously amenable to the prevailing standards.

But it is obvious that it is increasingly dangerous to yield to this inveterate tendency, however comfortable and respectable it may seem for the moment.

History, as H. G. Wells has so finely expressed it, is coming more and more to be "a race between education and catastrophe. Our internal policies and our economic and social ideas are profoundly vitiated at present by wrong and fantastic ideas of the origin and historical relationship of social classes. A sense of history as the common adventure of all mankind is as necessary for peace within as it is for peace between the nations." There can be no secure peace now but a common peace of the whole world; no prosperity but a general prosperity, and this for the simple reason that we are all now brought so near together and are so pathetically and intricately interdependent, that the old notions of noble isolation and national sovereignty are magnificently criminal.

In the bottom of their hearts, or the depths of their unconscious, do not the conservatively minded realize that their whole attitude toward the world and its betterment is based on an assumption that finds no least support in the Great Book of the Past? Does it not make plain that the "conservative," so far as he is consistent and lives up to his professions, is fatally in the wrong? The so-called "radical" is also almost always wrong, for no one can foresee the future. But he works on a right assumption—namely, that the future has so far always proved different from the past and that it will continue to do so. Some of us, indeed, see that the future is tending to become more and more rapidly and widely different from the past. The conservative himself furnishes the only illustration of his theory, and even that is highly inconclusive. His general frame of mind appears to remain constant, but he finds himself defending and rejecting very different things. The great issue may, according to the period, be a primeval taboo, the utterances of the Delphic oracle, the

Athanasian creed, the Inquisition, the geocentric theory, monarchy by the grace of God, witchcraft, slavery, war, capitalism, private property, or noble isolation. All of these tend to appear to the conservative under the aspect of eternity, but all of these things have come, many of them have gone, and the remainder would seem to be subject to undreamed-of modifications as time goes on. This is the teaching of the now unsealed book.

APPENDIX

Some Suggestions in Regard to Reading

IT may happen that among the readers of this essay there will be some who will ask how they can most readily get a clearer idea of the various newer ways of looking at mankind and the problems of the day. The following list of titles is furnished with a view of doing something to meet this demand. It is not a bibliography in the usual sense of the term. It is confined to rather short and readily understandable presentations appropriate to the overcrowded schedule upon which most of us have to operate. All the writers mentioned belong, however, to that rather small class whose opinions are worth considering, even if one reserves the imprescriptible right not to agree with all they say. There may well be better references than those with which I happen to be acquainted, and others quite as useful; but I can hardly imagine anyone, whatever his degree of information, unless he happens to be a specialist in the particular field, failing to gain something of value from any one of the volumes mentioned.

For the astounding revelations in regard to the fundamental nature of matter and the ways in which the modern chemist plays with it, see John Mills, *Within the Atom* (D. Van Nostrand Company), and Slosson, *Creative Chemistry* (The Century Company).

A general account of the evolutionary process will be found in Crampton, *The Doctrine of Evolution* (Columbia University Press), chaps. i-v. For our development as an individual from the egg see Conklin, *Heredity and Environment* (Princeton University Press).

The general scope of modern anthropology and the influence of this study on our notions of mankind as we now find it can be gathered from Goldenweiser, *Early Civilization, Introduction to Anthropology* (Knopf). This should be supplemented by the remarkable volume of essays by Franz Boas, *The Mind of Primitive Man* (Macmillan).

Of the more recent and easily available books relating to the reconstruction of philosophy and the newer conceptions in regard to mind and intelligence the following may be mentioned: Dewey, *Reconstruction in Philosophy* and *Human Nature and Conduct* (Holt); Woodworth, *Dynamic Psychology* (Columbia University Press); Trotter, *Instincts of the Herd in Peace and War* (Macmillan) —especially the first two sections, pp. 1–65; Bernard Hart, *The Psychology of Insanity* (Putnam), an admirable little introduction to the importance of abnormal mental conditions in understanding our usual thoughts and emotions; McDougall,

Social Psychology (J. W. Luce); Everett D. Martin, *The Behavior of Crowds* (Harpers); Edman, *Human Traits* (Houghton-Mifflin). For the so-called behavioristic interpretation of mankind, see Watson, *Psychology from the Standpoint of a Behaviorist* (Lippincott). Haldane, *Mechanism, Life, and Personality* (Dutton), is a short discussion of some of the most fundamental elements in our modern conception of life itself.

When it comes to gaining an idea of "Freudianism" and all the overwhelming discoveries, theories, and suggestions due to those who have busied themselves with the lasting effects of infantile and childish experiences, of hidden desires—sexual and otherwise, of "the Unconscious" and psychoanalysis, while there are many books, great and small, there would be no unanimity of opinion among those somewhat familiar with the subjects as to what should be recommended. It would be well if everyone could read in Havelock Ellis, *The Philosophy of Conflict* (Houghton-Mifflin), the essay (XVIII) on Freud and his influence. Wilfred Lay, *Man's Unconscious Conflict* (Dodd, Mead), is a popular exposition of psychoanalysis, and Tansley, *The New Psychology* (Dodd, Mead), likewise. Harvey O'Higgins, *The Secret Springs* (Harpers), reports, in a pleasing manner, some of the actual medical experiences of Dr. Edward Reede of Washington. But much of importance remains unsaid in all these little books, for which one would have to turn to Freud himself, his present and former disciples, his enemies, and the special contributions of investigators and practitioners in this new and essential field of psychological research and therapy.

Turning to the existing industrial system, its nature, defects, and recommendations for its reform, I may say that I think that relatively little is to be derived from the common run of economic textbooks. The following compendious volumes give an analysis of the situation and a consideration of the proposed remedies for existing evils and maladjustments: Veblen, *The Vested Interests and the Common Man*, also his *The Engineers and the Price System* (Huebsch); J. A. Hobson, *Democracy after the War* (Macmillan) and his more recent *Problems of a New World* (Macmillan); Tawney, *The Acquisitive Society* (Harcourt, Brace); Bertrand Russell, *Why Men Fight* (Century) and his *Proposed Roads to Freedom* (Holt), in which he describes clearly the history and aims of the various radical leaders and parties of recent times.

As for newer views and criticism of the modern state and political life in general, in addition to Mr. Hobson's books mentioned above, the following are of importance: Graham Wallas, *The Great Society* (Macmillan); Harold Laski, *Authority in the Modern State* and *Problems of Sovereignty* (Yale University Press); Walter Lippmann, *Preface to Politics* and *Drift and Mastery* (Holt).

J. Russell Smith, *The World's Food Resources*

(Holt), is a larger and more detailed discussion than most of those recommended above, but contains a number of general facts and comment of first-rate importance.

One who desires a highly thoughtful and scholarly review of the trend of religious thought in recent times should read McGiffert, *The Rise of Modern Religious Ideas* (Macmillan).